ENDORSEMENTS

"A heartfelt story of hope, commitment, and beauty from ashes."

- KAY BRATT, child advocate and author of
Silent Tears: A Journey of Hope in a Chinese Orphanage

"I want to bless *With an Open Heart*, as I believe it is in God's heart that we all love and care for the orphans of the world. Daniel's life was brief, but he died knowing he had a forever family that loved and fought for him until the very end. The true meaning of pure and lasting religion is told through Daniel's story."

- PAMELA COPE, author of *Jantsen's Gift*
and founder of Touch a Life Foundation

"*With an Open Heart* is a deeply moving story about a beautiful young soul that lives on after his body has departed. Daniel had a heart he couldn't live without, nor could he live with. God just needed him. This book takes you inside the Murphy family's loving journey with their little angel, Daniel."

- FRANK MCKINNEY, five-time bestselling author, including *The Tap*
and founder of The Caring House Project Foundation

"From the first page, I was drawn into this compelling and beautifully-written story. Ms. Murphy artfully and lovingly chronicles her family's shockingly short, yet profoundly powerful experience with a darling little boy and his staggering zest for life. Rather than a tragedy, the story of *With an Open Heart* is one of hope, faith and inspiration. A story so timely in this age of pessimism, many readers will find it life-altering. I did."

- CINDIE LEONARD, freelance writer and ghostwriter of *Laura's Story*

"This book is a celebration of one little boy's strong, happy spirit— one that prompted his Half the Sky nanny in Nanchang to write, 'I loved this beautiful boy at first sight,' and a spirit that inspired his forever mom in Florida to write *With an Open Heart*."

- PATRICIA KING, Half the Sky Foundation

"I am moved by *With an Open Heart*, and honored to recommend this inspiring story of adversity, courage, hope and love. When Daniel traveled from China to become part of the Murphy family, no one knew how serious his heart condition was—nor could anyone have guessed that in just four short months he would have such a profound impact on so many lives."

- BETH SMITH, Holt International Children's Services

REVISED EDITION

WITH AN OPEN

Heart

A true story of love, loss, and unexpected blessings, by

LISA MURPHY

with Marilyn Murray Willision

KINGDOM ♥ HEART
PUBLISHING

WITH AN OPEN HEART
REVISED EDITION
Follow the ongoing story: www.facebook.com/withanopenheartbook
Download the discussion guide: www.withanopenheartbook.com

DEDICATION

I dedicate this book to you, fellow adoptive Mamas...

For your obedience to follow Christ and for your willingness
to leap out of your comfort zones to love God's children
around the globe. I am especially grateful for you
Mamas who adopt children with uncertain futures,
yet you still choose to leap with faith against all odds.
You inspire me, and it is an honor to know you.

I dedicate this book to you, Mamas who have lost children...

I pray that you are divinely embraced during
your times of sorrow, and that your holes of grief
are filled with peace that only our Lord can give.
May your angels be near.

Table of Contents

Introduction

LIVE, LISTEN & LEAP

This is the story of Daniel – our first adopted son from China. Many of us believe that God has the power to move mountains. I know I do. One of our family's "mountains" happened to be our little boy whose given Chinese name, Weifeng, translates to "Great Mountain," and God moved him into our family from an orphanage halfway across the world. He experienced the love of a family and ultimately touched thousands of lives. In just four short months, Daniel's story created a not-to-be-forgotten faith movement in our community. Our hope is that you will take three things away from Daniel's inspiring story:

ONE - LIVE WITH AN OPEN HEART

Daniel's bright, unique spirit allowed him to handle even the toughest situations with courage and enthusiasm. He faced so many trials (both mental and physical), but Daniel fought through every single challenge and always ended up with a smile on his face. We should all aspire to live our lives as Daniel did.

TWO - LISTEN WITH AN OPEN HEART

This is also a story about our family's faith-filled experience and how the Lord wove His wonders through our adoption journey. It is a testament to how the grace of God gives each of us surprising strength to endure otherwise overwhelming trials. It is about how the Holy Spirit *whispers* to each of us every day. The question is – are our hearts open to hearing what He has to say? Are we truly listening to Him?

Now, I'm not in any way, shape, or form the "holier than thou" type, and I am far, far from perfect. But I do believe in God, I do believe in Jesus Christ, and I do believe in the Holy Spirit. In fact, I've seen them in action at various times in my life. It's important to me that readers of all faiths know up front that we are devoted disciples of Christ, and our Catholic faith played a pivotal role in Daniel's adoption. I understand that people with other spiritual beliefs may find it hard to resonate with our deep, personal relationship with Jesus Christ. But I hope that no one who reads Daniel's story feels excluded or offended because of our faith. This is, after all, one family's story.

THREE - LEAP WITH AN OPEN HEART

The phrase *leap of faith* was coined for a reason and is defined as "an act or instance of accepting or trusting in something that cannot readily be seen or proven." Please don't be afraid to take risks in order to accomplish your calling in this life. I truly hope you follow your heart and live your life with the joy and spiritual abundance you were designed to have, and given the freedom to choose. When we took our leap of faith to bring Daniel, or any of our children home, we had no idea what the consequences would be. God called us, and we simply answered. I can't even begin to imagine life without Daniel had we not taken that leap and answered that call from above. Opening our hearts to him was a gift – one that was totally worth the risk.

As I see it, God tests all of us in ways that make us better and bring us closer to Him. If we don't allow ourselves to be stretched, then how will we ever experience the grace and reward of growing in His love? We won't. Trust God. Open your heart and take chances. Allow yourself to be stretched in His ways.

There is an ancient Chinese belief that states, "An invisible red thread connects those who are destined to meet, regardless of time, place, or circumstance. The thread may stretch or tangle, but it will never break." This story is where part of *our* thread became stretched and tangled, but, as that ancient belief states, "it will *never* break."

Chapter One

MATCHED WITH A SON

From time to time, during a discussion about adoption, someone will ask, "Why China?" as if my husband, Jimmy, and I have treaded over the line of our American patriotism. This question always allows us to answer – honestly – "Because that's where God told us to go." We had explored domestic adoption possibilities, as well as other countries and their adoption programs, but God clearly called us to go to China. And does it really matter where our children are born when there are, literally, millions of children in the world who wish for the one seemingly simple thing that most of us take for granted – a family?

I believe that God planted a seed in my husband, Jimmy, back in ninth grade at Clawson High School (in Clawson, Michigan) when his class learned about the "dying rooms" in China where baby girls were abandoned and left to die. Those babies basically cried themselves to sleep and never woke up. Back then, Chinese orphans had no hope. Jimmy never forgot that lesson, and once the subject of adoption came to the table in our home, he knew right away where he wanted to go – directly to China. Do not pass "Go." Do not collect $200.

Adoption is a funny thing. You work and work through mountains of documentation, forms, and red tape while you simultaneously wait and wait some more. It gives new meaning to the word *patience,* and it seems like a never-ending process – that is, until your child is placed into your arms. Then, much like suffering through the labor pains of childbirth, by the grace of God you get through it, and the agony you endured to get there is forgotten. One day, all of a sudden, your heart *begs* to adopt again. Sometimes, I feel like I could be one of those old women who brings a hundred cats into her home – but with me, it would be children. I feel like I could adopt over and over again simply because the reward is so great. The bond of adoption is so miraculous that it makes one long for more.

When my husband and I brought our daughter, Madi, home from China in September of 2006 (at the tender age of one-year), adopting another child was not really in our plans. In fact, it wasn't even a thought. We were completely satisfied with our one little bundle of joy. However, it only took about two years for the Holy Spirit to start working on us again, and in early 2008, Jimmy and I began thinking about adopting a sibling (with a common heritage) for Madi to grow up with. After all, Jimmy and I each have a sibling with whom we shared our childhoods.

The idea started to escalate in January, 2008, when we received a phone call one night from Aunt Karen (my husband's aunt from Georgia). She was at a Christian music concert, which we could hear rumbling loudly in the background. She could barely contain her enthusiasm and screamed into the phone that Shaohannah's Hope could help us adopt a second child. She was at a Steven Curtis Chapman concert (he's the co-founder of Show Hope with his wife, Mary Beth). That was the first I'd heard of this organization, but a seed had been planted.

When Jimmy and I continued to explore the possibilities, a few interesting discussions took place that further influenced our decision. Our thirteen-year-old niece and godchild, Kelsey, was visiting from Michigan that February, and we were discussing the idea of another adoption in our family.

"Aunt Lisa, do you want to know what I think?" Kelsey asked. I adore my niece and value her opinion tremendously.

"Yes, I do, Kelsey. Please tell me your thoughts on this," I replied while holding my breath. Since Kelsey is an only child, I truly had no idea which direction her thoughts were headed.

Without reservation, Kelsey said, "If there's one thing I wish I'd had when I was growing up, it would have been a brother or a sister. I think you should do it *for Madi*." It was overwhelming to hear such an honest and heartfelt commentary on the subject, especially coming from Kelsey's perspective.

That was a particularly motivating moment, and I quickly found myself – once again – researching adoption agencies. This time, we were guided to Holt International Children's Services, a different agency than we'd used to bring Madi home. The name had always resonated with me as "Holt" is a family name in my Mother's Danish lineage, and we had heard they were a solid and reputable organization. Holt International is a Christian organization that was founded over fifty years ago and continues to be a world leader in international adoption and child welfare programs. Holt is dedicated to carrying out God's plan for every child to have a permanent, loving family. Another contributing factor to our choice was that our home study social worker, Amy, whom we completely adore, was on Holt's list of approved agencies. I completed the application, and so the process began.

Within a couple of weeks, our Holt agent, Beth, called with a few additional questions. She said, "I have good news and bad news. Which do you want first?" Oh, how I hated the sound of that question! My heart skipped a few beats as I responded, "The bad news."

Beth went on, "Well, the bad news is that the wait for healthy infant girls in China has significantly increased, and families have now been waiting over three years for referrals. But the good news is that on your application, you indicated that you would be open to a child with a minor medical condition." Beth continued, "Well there are many children in China with minor special needs who need families – both boys and girls – so the good news is that the referral time would be much quicker. And you could end up with a child of either gender!"

These were both important considerations for us. The quicker timeframe was a major bonus because my husband and I were both over forty years old. Jimmy (who, in my opinion, is one of the most humorous people on earth) has always joked that it's important to raise our kids before he's old enough to use a walker. Plus, we also wanted to experience the same element of surprise that we would have had with a pregnancy – not knowing ahead of time which gift God would give us. I told Beth that I would discuss everything with my husband and get back to her.

That evening before bed, I nervously rambled on to Jimmy about every detail of my conversation with Beth and hoped that we were on the same page. In my mind, I had already decided that this was going to happen. Jimmy said nothing. Knowing that it was more to digest than eating ten pizzas, I left it alone, and we went to sleep. The subject stayed on the outer fringe of conversation the next day. I desperately wanted to ask Jimmy how he felt, but I didn't want to push him or rush his decision, so I avoided the topic altogether.

That afternoon, on the way over to the house of close friends, Jimmy finally offered his two cents, "I thought about what you told me last night." For the second time in two days, my heart skipped a few beats. "And…I think we should go for it," he said with conviction.

It took me a minute to believe that my ears weren't deceiving me. My joy was so great that I could have jumped up and down and screamed at the top of my lungs. In fact, maybe I did! Praise the Lord, Jimmy and I were on the same page.

Oddly enough, that initial commitment was the most difficult part of the entire process. The second most difficult part was completing our "minor medical conditions checklist." Combing through a long list of physical challenges (while trying to figure out which ones are acceptable to you) is an arduous and painful process because it makes you examine everything about your heart and soul. Having to say "no" to a child is difficult enough, but what a guilt-ridden process it is to sit there and eliminate specific medical conditions knowing that those children need families, too.

Our social worker, Amy, gave us a priceless piece of advice. She said, "Listen – you need to be brutally honest with yourselves. There is no child attached to this report, and it's better to be honest about what is or isn't acceptable up front rather than turn a child's referral down – *that* is when you are truly faced with the meaning of *difficult.*"

So, with much contemplation, we went through each condition one by one, researched each of them on the internet, and narrowed down the list of what we felt we could handle. We weren't sure why, but we continuously found ourselves saying "yes" to heart conditions on the medical conditions checklist. There were many other medical ailments that may have been less challenging, but heart conditions kept coming back to us as something we could openly accept.

As we began sharing our decision with others close to us, a few reasons heart conditions had been on our radar became apparent. We discovered that our home study social worker, Amy, had several heart conditions that had been surgically corrected throughout her life, even into adulthood. And one of our best friends, Lisa, was born with Tetralogy of Fallot and had been a "blue baby" (I'll explain more about that later). She didn't have her open heart surgery until she was nine years old which is considered quite late by medical standards, yet Lisa is still here and in our lives today to talk about it. Our dear friend, Carol, who is truly like a sister to us, was also born with Tetralogy of Fallot. She, too, had open-heart surgery as a child, and we are blessed to have her in our lives today. Then, there is little Paige, our friends' daughter, who had heart surgery during her first months of life and continues to beat the odds with her strong fighting spirit.

When Jimmy and I took it all in, we realized that it was no accident that heart conditions resonated with us so deeply. God had placed all of these amazing people in our lives for a reason. We were surrounded by success stories, and we were mentally and spiritually prepared to take this on.

It took about one year to prepare our adoption dossier, which consists of a thorough and complex collection of original birth and marriage certificates, background checks with law enforcement agencies, references from employers and friends, detailed financial statements, visitations and reports from an authorized home study agency, and proof of good physical health. There were also applications to file with the U.S. Government. Once collected, all of these documents must be notarized, certified by the state, and then authenticated by the Chinese Embassy. The dossier then goes back to the adoption agency for review and is ultimately shipped to the officials in Beijing, China where it is logged in. We worked feverishly throughout the year to complete that documentation process and were thrilled to receive our I-800A (Application for Determination of Suitability to Adopt a Child from a Convention

Country) approval in December, 2008, after a four-month wait. And on my birthday – January 28th – we received the blessed gift of an email from our adoption agency reporting the wonderful news that our dossier looked "good to go." It was shipped off to China the very next day and was logged in shortly thereafter.

I vividly remember the day I received the phone call from Holt with news of a referral. It was July 7th, 2009, and I was returning from errands to the grocery store and the bank. Madi and my friend Sherril's daughter, Julianna, were in the back seat of our minivan. I answered my cell phone and heard the voice of Beth, our Holt agent, telling me that they had a little boy who needed a home. I'll never forget that moment as tears welled up in my eyes, and I could barely speak – or drive, for that matter!

Here's when I should back up about two weeks to June 24th, which was the day my mother-in-law (whom I'll refer to as Grandma Pauline) passed away. She'd had a long, drawn-out battle with uterine cancer, and her body finally succumbed to the struggle. Grandma Pauline had been incredibly involved in Madi's life, and they had been very, very close. Jimmy and I had been mentally bracing ourselves for this loss, but how do you possibly prepare a three-year old child to enter this territory?

The morning that we lost Grandma Pauline, Jimmy and I went in Madi's bedroom to break the news to her. We had a couple of treasures to give Madi for keeps – the stuffed dog, Willy, that Madi had lovingly given her Grandma to keep her company in the hospital, and a wind-up musical cross that Madi had picked out in the hospital gift shop. I remember the day we bought it. Madi marched into the gift shop and made a beeline right to that cross. There must have been at least fifty different music boxes, but Madi went straight for the cross. There was no way I could deny her. I didn't even realize that it was a music box until we took it to the register, and the clerk wound it up for us. I was stunned when it played the song "Memories" from the musical "Cats," which was the same tune that Madi's music box at home played. It was beautifully appropriate, and Grandma Pauline had cherished it.

That morning in Madi's bedroom, as Jimmy and I handed over those treasures to her, we also had to conjure up the right words to explain that Grandma had gone to Heaven. As the three of us cried together, all huddled on her bed, Jimmy and I told our daughter that Grandma had an important job to do – she was going to find us a baby.

So, when the phone rang two weeks later with our news of a baby, I knew in my heart that he was the one. I tried like mad to keep my composure, especially with the kids in the car. I drove straight home and ran inside the house to call Jimmy, praying all the while that after mentally enduring so much with the loss of his mother, he would feel the same way. My husband was cautiously optimistic and agreed that we should pursue more information. I sensed that he could barely wait to get home.

Later that day, we were emailed the file about Weifeng Hong, a baby boy from Nanchang in China's Jiangxi province, born February 2nd, 2008. This child, born on Groundhog Day, had multiple heart conditions – all of which sounded grave – but what did we know? In hindsight, ignorance was bliss.

We were told that he had been found outside the gates of a prominent residential community. There was no birth note with him. He had been sent to the Nanchang Social Welfare Institute by the public security bureau on September 2nd, 2008, and the children's department in the Institute estimated his date of birth and named him. On admission, he was about seven months old.

The report described him as a lovely and fat little boy, with big bright eyes and white skin. His development was normal, and his personality sounded perfect to us. How does one possibly give up their child after seven months of togetherness? It still tortures my heart to think about it. Whoever placed him there *must have* loved him and cared about him. It is likely that they could not provide the medical care that he needed in a culture where medical needs and visible differences are a tremendous burden, and – in many cases – also viewed as a curse.

Jimmy and I read his file over and over just wanting to soak up every detail and know him more intimately. We stared at his pictures and intensely studied every beautiful detail. Those big, brown eyes were calling for us to come back to China. For those of you who haven't adopted a child, the idea of falling in love with a photo may sound strange. But I can assure you that it actually happens. Perhaps it is the same feeling that biological parents experience when they see the first ultrasound image of their unborn baby – that pure love that swells into a tidal wave of hopes and dreams.

Referral photo of Weifeng Hong

Our friends, Molly and Todd, had recently gone through heart surgeries with their daughter, Paige, whom I mentioned previously. Our friend, Sherril, had paid particularly close attention to her medical care and knew exactly the right direction in which to point us. The next day, I contacted their pediatric cardiologist to make an appointment. I felt overwhelmed about our time constraint with a letter of intent. The adoption agency needed a firm "yes" in writing within a day or two, so time was of the essence. But still, we wanted to be cautious and have at least one solid medical opinion. Fortunately, the cardiologist's office could not have been kinder.

The office administrator evidently heard the urgency in my voice and asked, "Can you be here tomorrow at 3:00?"

I was blown away. "Of course, we will!" I replied with a surge of relief. The next day, the cardiologist spent over an hour with Jimmy and me (at his expense) reviewing the file and explaining this baby's condition to us. The news sounded serious, but what we heard was *hope* – for this child, *there was hope.*

The medical records from China indicated that our perfect match had Tetralogy of Fallot, which meant that he had four major heart defects. I am by no stretch a medical expert, but to my understanding, these were the conditions that we were facing: He had pulmonary atresia – the congenital absence of a pulmonary opening. In pulmonary atresia, the pulmonary valve, which is normally located between the right ventricle and the pulmonary artery, is abnormal and doesn't open. This means that oxygen-poor blood can't flow forward from the right ventricle to the lungs to get oxygenated. Medical and surgical interventions are required since the oxygen-poor blood cannot meet the body's demands, and this situation cannot support long life.

The baby also had a ventricular septal defect (VSD). This is a hole in the heart wall (septum) that separates the two ventricles.

The hole is usually large and allows oxygen-poor blood in the right ventricle to pass through and mix with oxygen-rich blood in the left ventricle. This poorly oxygenated blood is then pumped out of the left ventricle to the rest of the body. The body gets some oxygen, but not all that it needs. This lack of oxygen in the blood causes cyanosis or a bluish appearance to the skin, thus the term "blue baby."

The other two defects, we were told, really couldn't be repaired. He had an *overriding aorta,* which is an abnormal positioning of the aorta, and there was *significant thickening of the right atrium* of his heart. Due to the narrowing or blockage of the pulmonary valve, there was a restriction to blood outflow that caused an increase in right ventricular work and pressure, leading to right ventricular thickening. Because he had lived with this condition since birth, his body had compensated accordingly in order to survive. Though he did not require oxygen therapy, the baby's oxygen saturation levels were in the seventies at rest, which is quite low.

In the United States, it is common to have these types of major heart surgeries during the first six months of life in order to avoid wear and tear on the body as it begins to compensate. The cardiologist explained to us that as he grew, the baby would likely need several surgeries during the course of his life. He would need at least one open heart surgery, probably more down the road.

That trip to the pediatric cardiologist sealed the deal for Jimmy and me. As the doctor provided us with the details of a seemingly solid plan to repair the baby's heart – through surgeries, therapies and medical procedures throughout his life – we did not hear "impossible," nor did we choose to. In our minds, we heard only words of "hope." So, we signed the papers that same day and immediately faxed them to Holt to lock the file.

Chapter Two

PREPARING FOR TRAVEL

Shortly after Grandma Pauline had passed away, we found – in a box in our garage – a beautiful bell that we had totally forgotten about. For a short time (back in 2003 or so), I'd represented a company that made beautiful copper bells, and this was one of my sales samples that had ended up collecting dust once I switched gears and changed careers during tough economic times. The copper patina bell was mysteriously appropriate for our family at that time, since it was a "remembrance bell" with a peace bird perched at its top. Because the sound of the bell was remarkably soothing, we attached it to Madi's play structure in the backyard.

I bring this up because we first noticed that bell really ringing furiously whenever we discussed the possibility of adopting this baby. I know that sounds certifiable, but Jimmy and I both became convinced that it was Grandma Pauline's way of communicating with us. The intriguing part was that we both felt it very strongly, and we each noticed it happening on separate occasions. Knowing just how crazy it sounded, we were both reluctant to mention it to each other. In fact, I can't recall which one of us actually voiced our confession first, but we were obviously shocked to discover this shared feeling. As we would sit in the backyard discussing the baby's heart condition and questioning whether or not we could meet his needs sufficiently, the bell would ring as if to answer our concerns and assure us that everything would be okay. We named it "Grandma's Bell," and I swear that it beckoned us to bring little Weifeng into our home just like the Pied Piper.

Jimmy and I spent the next month keeping our decision secret from most of our acquaintances but shared the pertinent information sparingly with family and close friends. Though we were prepared to go down this new road, we weren't sure how our family members felt about us bringing a child with significant special needs into our lives. After all, our decision would directly affect their lives, too. To some, we knew the thought seemed just too plain scary and uncomfortable to initially accept. We also wanted to protect Madi until we were absolutely certain that this adoption was going to happen, so we chose to keep things quiet.

My husband and I met with our social worker and had several conference calls in the next few weeks to talk us through this child's condition just to be sure we were ready to accept this calling that had been offered to us. We went from certain to uncertain and back, and even though fear reared its ugly head at times, deep down in our hearts we knew that we would move forward.

This is the beginning of the journey that we embarked on with our son. One month after we received his file, I asked Jimmy, "Should we show the pictures to Madi?" He nodded, and we nervously called our daughter to come look at the pictures of her little brother on our computer. We just couldn't wait any longer and pretend that we didn't want this. Jimmy and I both knew that once the world, and Madi, had been told about our baby, there would be no turning back. Upon hearing our news, Madi was excited beyond our expectations and ran wildly through the house declaring all the many things she would teach him! She could hardly wait to be his big sister.

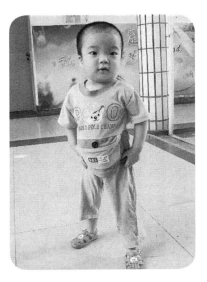

Weifeng in China at 18 months old

Initially, when we told my parents (affectionately known to Madi as "Bubba" and "Grandpa") about their new grandson, we had planned to name him Max. In fact, the whole time that we reviewed his file and spoke about him, he was Max. That is, until the Holy Spirit prompted us to name him Daniel.

Jimmy's best friend in college, Daniel (Danny) Foreman, had just passed away in February 2009. In his twenties, Danny had fought Hodgkin's disease, a form of cancer that he successfully overcame. But the toll radiation took on his body was severe. His heart was hardened by scar tissue and his liver was failing, too. On New Year's Eve of 2008, Danny was admitted to the University of Pittsburgh Medical Center (UPMC), as he was finally matched with a donor for a double-organ transplant. For months, if not years, this was something the family had hoped, prayed, and waited for. The transplant was reason to celebrate a chance at a renewed life for Danny. Unfortunately for all who loved him, the organ transplant was not successful. And Danny's body constantly struggled to accept the new organs until he finally lost his fight.

Our decision to name our son "Daniel" was two-fold. First, it was to honor Daniel Foreman as a dear friend, but it was also because we believed that our son, Daniel, would live for the very reason that Danny Foreman had not – because of his heart. We presumed that our Daniel's heart surgery would be successful, and that he would live a long, happy life and carry on the great name of a life-loving friend.

Throughout the next few months, Jimmy and I began the "nesting" stage again, and a bevy of paperwork ensued. I was busy handling all of the details in writing while working diligently to get all necessary approvals underway and completed. Things started to happen really fast, and though we weren't sure when our travel would take place, we hoped that it would be in the next few months given Daniel's serious medical condition.

The wait became painful. Month after month, we questioned the adoption agency. We questioned United States Citizenship and Immigration Services about our approvals, too. It didn't matter. We were exasperated, and we became terribly frustrated by our government. Why were we the only people in the world who seemed to feel a sense of urgency here? We just couldn't understand why they couldn't move things along when this poor little guy was a million miles away, and his life was becoming more tenuous by the day. Jimmy and I were finally forced to accept the reality that this process was out of our control – *totally* out of our hands. Both of us realized that we had to relinquish all control to God, and with that, we were able to find some peace as we trudged through the paperwork, one filing at a time.

During that long and grueling waiting period, Jimmy and I had introduced the idea of travel to Grandpa Murphy (Jimmy's father). We had been working on him for a while, and we were so hopeful that he would make the decision to go to China with us to bring Daniel home. It would be perfect if he could accompany us, especially since we felt so strongly about Grandma Pauline's divine involvement with finding Daniel.

When Jimmy's father finally said yes, we were ecstatic and knew that Grandpa Murphy would experience the trip of a lifetime. We were blessed that my parents (Bubba and Grandpa) had traveled to China with us to bring Madi home. It had been such an amazing experience for them, and it was extra special to have loving, supportive parents present for us. Since my mom and dad had made the trip with us before, they graciously offered to stay at our house and take care of Madi and our cats this time. Jimmy and I knew that Madi would be more comfortable at home, and we also knew that she would be comfortable with Bubba and Grandpa caring for her. Our daughter had been assigned the important responsibility of planning the party for our arrival home, and time would fly for her as she remained busy with all her activities.

The plans were shaping up perfectly, and I posted about our first major milestone – LOA (Letter of Acceptance) from China – on our family blog:

ONE STEP CLOSER | Sept. 12, 2009

We received our LOA (Letter of Acceptance) from China this week! We were told that this could take anywhere from 6 weeks to 4.5 months. Thankfully, we had it in our hands in exactly 2 months. We signed all the necessary documents, and sent the package to Holt via FedEx for Monday arrival. We also included a soft photo book for them to send to Daniel in China, so he can begin studying the faces of his new family. This week, we learned of a new step in the process that we hadn't been required to do the first time around. We have to take 10 hours of parenting classes to satisfy the Hague requirements! Hello! Has anyone seen our daughter Madi lately? I'd like to think we're doing okay over here!

Actually, we're okay with it. We realize that they do this for the safety and protection of the children. Jimmy and I started the online courses last night, and they are pretty cool. I think the Lord prepares us in certain ways, and maybe this time around we will need more preparation than we did for Madi. The circumstances are obviously very different. So, thanks for the prayers! Please keep them up! The next step we need to complete is to get our approvals from USCIS. We are hoping that this will take less than a month. Estimated travel date: still too early to tell!

During that "paper chase" phase of our adoption, I took Madi with me to the Post Office one day to mail some of our documents. The contents of the envelope escapes me now (probably the signed Letter of Acceptance), but I had been so excited to mail this packet and kept telling her that we needed to take care of these papers to get the baby. She could see that – based on my urgency – this envelope was a top priority as we hustled into the post office line and waited somewhat patiently for our turn.

As we pulled away from the Post Office, Madi was totally perplexed and asked, "Mommy, *where is Daniel?* I thought we came here to pick him up!"

It took me a minute to realize what had happened. Poor Madi was expecting to bring her little brother home that very day. She was so disappointed when we left the Post Office without Daniel!

Another one of the tricky parts about adoption paperwork is that many of the documents expire at different times during the process. Fingerprint clearances, a requirement of Homeland Security, are valid for only 15 months. Ours had expired on October 29th, 2009, and we were sent new appointment notices, which I had hastily added to our calendar. We were ready to leave for our appointments when I glanced at the document and felt all of the blood rush from my body. How could that paper have read November 2nd when it was already November 3rd? *I had written the wrong day down on the calendar* – that's how!

I instantly fell into a panic, especially when my eyes caught the disclaimer which stated, "If you fail to make your appearance, your case will be abandoned." Oh my dear Lord! The panic set in deeper. Thank God that Jimmy – who is usually level-headed when I am not – was there to calm me down.

Madi started to get upset and began to shout, "Daddy, I want our baby! I want our baby!" I dialed up our USCIS case worker, Matthew, and he calmly recommended that we show up at the support center anyhow to see what would happen. So we did exactly as he suggested. We drove up to Royal Palm Beach, about forty-five minutes away from our home, and much to our Murphy's Law surprise, they swept us in and out without a single hiccup. We were fingerprinted and out the door in 15 minutes!

We continued to wait for our travel approval with the knowledge that once we received it, Jimmy and I would be on to the final step of planning our travel arrangements. On November 5th, 2009, we received a welcome update from Holt on Daniel's progress! As one might imagine, any scrap of information about your waiting child is pure treasure. We were smiling after we read the update because it sure sounded as if Daniel had been holding his own! The update read:

> He exhibits well-developed eye accommodation. He can walk up and down stairs one at a time with pauses. He can turn door knobs and climb on furniture. He chews more effectively. He walks and runs with a stiff gait and wide stance. He can use a spoon, but will spill. He can kick a ball in front of him without support. He has daytime bladder and bowel control, but nighttime control not complete. He doesn't talk too much. He speaks only some simple words such as "Ba Ba" which means Dad and "Ma Ma" which means Mom. He helps to undress and tries to button. He wants to hoard and not share his favorite toys. If others take his favorite toys away, he will try to get it back. His favorite toy is a set of toy kitchen and cookware. He gets along well with other children. But sometimes he will compete for toys with others.

On New Year's Eve, Jimmy and I received the joyous, long-awaited confirmation that we would leave for China on January 20th, 2010 to bring our son home. It was so surreal. The two of us enjoyed a quiet, romantic New Year's Eve together on our back patio and celebrated our news over a filet mignon dinner and a good bottle of red wine. The details of our travel timeline came as such a huge relief. Jimmy and I had both been so concerned that our trip would be further delayed because of Chinese New Year celebrations, in which the entire country literally shuts down for a couple of weeks. Thankfully, Holt had managed to squeeze us into the last group of travelers before the holiday.

For months, we had carried around Daniel's picture, showing him off to whoever cared to know about him and, basically, to anyone who would listen. Madi would bring his picture to church with us, and together we would pray for his health and safety until we could get to him. We were over the moon at the idea of starting the New Year in such a meaningful way. It almost seemed like a dream to Jimmy and me. As an added bonus, I would be spending my 43rd birthday in China with our son, and we would also be celebrating his 2nd birthday together in his homeland.

The first few weeks of our new year were spent hustling around to get Daniel's room ready and prepare for our trip. There was much to be done in such a short time, because we had put travel preparations on hold until we knew for sure that our itinerary was in stone. The door to our son's bedroom had been shut for months, and now the idea of a new life in that room brought new life into our entire home. We began receiving mountains of hand-me-down clothing and toys. Thanks to the overwhelming generosity of friends, we never had to buy Daniel one stitch of clothing.

Our Mei Mei group (it means "Little Sister" in Chinese, and consists of about ten gorgeous little girls adopted from China) gave Madi and me an intimate baby shower and dinner to celebrate. It was perfect timing for me to soak up last-minute advice about travel and packing, which really brought forth the excitement and anticipation of our impending journey. Jimmy and I had forgotten an awful lot since our first adoption experience, and the group certainly reminded me of a few good tips. They are such a wonderful collection of loving families, and they were so excited to welcome the first Di Di ("Little Brother" in Chinese) to our group!

The last week before we traveled was, in a way, almost beautiful and sad at the same time with the realization that our family dynamic was about to change forever. Jimmy and I fully embraced the idea of having another family member to love, but at the same time, we cherished every solitary moment we had alone with Madi – knowing that our time with her would soon be shared with another. Neither Jimmy nor I had ever been away from Madi for such a lengthy time, and we knew that being away from each other for over two weeks was going to be tough on her, and on us. But we also knew – all of us – that this extraordinary trip to bring home our son was something we simply had to do.

Madi and Mommy just before our trip

Chapter Three

THE BEGINNING OF OUR JOURNEY

Enjoying my relatively apolitical life in sunny South Florida, I did not realize that China censored the internet. Honestly, I'd never given it a single thought. (Oops.) I actually made the discovery when I wasn't able to access my blog when we arrived in China. I became concerned because I'd promised so many friends and family members that we would post about our journey, and provide regular updates.

Thank God for my brother, Andrew, who became an administrator (and guest blogger) on our account. I emailed Andrew the updates regularly, and then he would post them for me. We had a great system worked out, and my brother actually did all of our blog posting during our trip back to China. Without Andrew's help, our journey to Daniel would never have been shared with our friends and family back at home. Jimmy and I will always be grateful to him for his efforts. Everyone needs an Andrew in their life!

WE MADE IT! | January 22, 2010

We arrived in Beijing yesterday afternoon. The flight was smooth; albeit — at 13:45 hours — a long one! At the airport, we met up with our tour guide, and four other adoptive families who are also adopting boys with medical conditions. Our hotel is surprisingly nice, in fact nicer than our last trip to China. Once we checked in, we decided to venture out for a Peking duck dinner in the middle of downtown Beijing, which is very safe. Thank goodness our dear friends lent us some warm clothing accessories, because it's freezing here! A warm and satisfying dinner was precisely the medicine we needed.

Afterwards, a sleeping pill helped me acclimate to the time change, which by the way is thirteen hours ahead of most of you. Yes, I am writing to you from tomorrow! This morning we woke up very early, and went downstairs for a breakfast of dumplings, noodles & a few other interesting things. Nothing like starting the day the Chinese way! Then our tour bus took us to the Great Wall of China. They've obviously cleaned things up around here (in preparation for the 2008 Olympics) because we've had blue skies so far. On our last trip, all we saw was smog. We were very proud of Grandpa Murphy, who climbed the Wall without much of a struggle at all.

After lunch, our guide took us to Hutong Lane, which has the oldest communal living spaces in Beijing. We toured on rickshaws! You should see what 3.5 million dollars buys you here. Without even a toilet in the house! The homeowner was really kind and gracious to take us in and show us where her family was raised for many generations. They truly are kind people here. It wouldn't be a Murphy day without something crazy happening. Our rickshaw bumped into the rickshaw in front of us – twice! The two drivers were yelling at each other like crazy. No whiplash to report, thankfully.

Now we are back at the hotel sipping a cold beer and contemplating dinner plans. We were told about a good restaurant next door to the hotel that serves really spicy food. In fact, so spicy that they won't serve some of it to tourists! We also plan to hit the open-air food market, with no plans to eat the scorpion skewers, of course.

We already miss Madi tremendously. Bubba has been so wonderful to keep us updated on her, and she is handling everything like a champ, as usual. We have been able to communicate with Madi through Skype on a daily basis, though the time difference makes it tough to connect. Here is an email Mom sent in Madi's words. I don't have to tell you what a sobbing mess I was when I read it:

Dear Mommy,

I miss you. I hope I see you. I know I am going to be a big sister, and I hope you come home soon. I really want to see my little brother. I know I won't see him very soon, but wish I could see him tomorrow. I really miss you, Mommy and Daddy. I hope Daniel will be safe. And I hope you have a great trip. I give you hugs and kisses, dear Mommy, Daddy and DJ. That's all. Now send it.

One of the wonderful families we bonded with was also back in China to adopt their son this time. They'd brought along their adorable six-year old daughter, Jaeden, who had been adopted from China years before. It sounds so silly, but that beautiful little Chinese girl reminded me so much of Madi that I felt compelled to talk to her and hug her every chance I could. It was merely the beginning of our trip, and Jimmy and I already missed Madi so much.

On January 22nd, our precious daughter sent us another priceless email message. We began to look so forward to receiving her messages. They made us laugh, and they made us cry. They made us all the more grateful to have that little girl at home waiting for us to return.

Dear Mommy and Daddy,

I miss you very much. I hope you have a great landing.

I hope D. J. is safe. I hope Daniel likes his cake. We will plan a party, and I hope Daniel likes it. Bubba and I played in the Fort yesterday. I climbed the rope up the slide seven times. We might eat all the tomatoes. They are way good. They are sweet 100. You're welcome back. We will have a very good dinner because we will celebrate Daniel. I ate chicken pot pie and lima beans last night. Why did you not buy corn? That's so funny :-) We might have flowers. And we will have decorations and balloons. I'm helping Bubba a lot making the beds. I'm having a great time with Bubba. Now send it.

Chapter Four

CLOSER TO TOGETHER

Our emotions were running high as Jimmy and I prepared our hearts for a new reality. This blog post summed it up well.

TOMORROW IS GOTCHA DAY | January 23, 2010

Here it is. We've almost arrived at the moment we've been waiting so long for. Tomorrow is Gotcha Day. Tomorrow they place Daniel in our arms. He'll be ours forever, and our family will be one family member richer. How did we get here? Wow. We started this process two years ago. We waited. We trusted God. And here we are. Yes, this is happening tomorrow, and our hearts feel fuller every minute that we get closer to meeting him.

This morning is our 3-hour orientation meeting with Holt. We found out that there will be 63 attendees, so our group is larger than we thought! We were told that some of us will receive updates on our children and, sadly, some of us will not. We hope to be amongst the lucky ones, so we can see how our little guy is doing. After our meeting we are going to Tiananmen Square and the Forbidden City for touring. The guys have decided to hit Beijing's Irish Pub tonight. They want a t-shirt! Our flight leaves tomorrow morning. I will try to post again this evening depending on our timing.

The very next day, *we were* one of the couples lucky enough to receive a precious book of updated information about Daniel in our meeting! We also received four new photos of him, and we were overcome with joy. We hadn't known what to expect, and Daniel looked great! He looked very full and well fed, and the information we were given indicated that his height and weight were on track, too. Our only concern was a certain seriousness, or perhaps sadness, that we detected in his eyes.

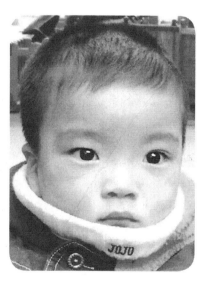

Weifeng's update photo

Jimmy and I received one bit of surprising information about our son's care. We were under the impression that he'd been living in the orphanage the whole time we were waiting to bring him home. But, apparently, he had been living in a Holt-sponsored group home within the orphanage since August 2009, and before that he had been part of a Half the Sky care center! Half the Sky Foundation is a charitable organization that helps assist orphans in China. We had donated to them in the past, and here, without us knowing, they had helped our own son! We were grateful (and lucky) that it seemed he had been in very good care.

That day in Beijing was packed full of touring. It was total déjà vu from our trip before to bring Madi home. As Jimmy and I walked around touring the ancient and historic Forbidden City and Tiananmen Square, we exchanged anxious glances, and we both found it very difficult to concentrate on anything but the next day – our Gotcha Day with Daniel. Our emotions were swinging like a pendulum. It was exactly how we'd felt – three years prior – right before we were united with Madi. The three of us hoped for a good night's sleep, since our flight was scheduled to depart Beijing the next morning at 11:30 a.m., and would arrive in Jiangxi province at 2:00 p.m. We would be united with Daniel at approximately 4:00 p.m. in our hotel that afternoon.

I'd heard that there was a Catholic Church about five minutes away from our hotel in Beijing, and ever since we'd arrived, I desperately wanted to see it. Before checkout that morning, we were ahead of schedule, so Jimmy and I made a split-second decision to take a quick walk to find the Wangfujing Catholic Church – the "East Church." We intended to pop in and, if nothing else, say a quick prayer. When we entered the magnificent and palatial structure, which dates back to 1655, the most breathtaking Mass was taking place – in Mandarin – and the choir sounded like a band of angels. We were there in time to offer peace to everyone around us. In China, it is tradition to bow to each other instead of shaking hands as we do here in the United States. We were also there in time to take communion, where hosts of rice were used. It was truly comforting to know that no matter where you are in the world, you are always *at home* in the presence of Jesus Christ. What a joyous way to start such a special day.

Chapter Five

HE IS OURS

The hours leading up to what adoptive families refer to as "Gotcha Day" seem surreal. The adoption process, in whole, takes so long, but then – before you blink – you have almost arrived at that life-changing moment when you are about to meet your child for the first time – a union that will transform souls.

HE IS OURS | January 24, 2010

All day long, I was asking myself wrenching questions like, "What if he rejects me?" If I remember correctly, that's a pretty normal thought process.

We arrived in Nanchang, which we discovered means "Hero," at approximately 3:30 p.m. Our guide, Lisa, told us that we should come up to the meeting room on the 20th floor at 4:30. For the hour in between, we were busy unpacking, trying to get the computer to work, packing our diaper bag, assembling gifts for the officials, doing anything to keep busy!

Lisa called us at 4:15 to say that Daniel had arrived, and we should come up. And so the nerves set in. We went upstairs to hear lots of crying. Fortunately for us, it was the twin baby girls in our group. We walked in the room and laid eyes on him and then approached him very cautiously. He was being held by the orphanage director. We spoke to him a little bit, and then she held him out to me. Initially, it seemed that he was frightened, and tears streamed down his sweet little face. I reassured him that everything would be okay. And he held on tight. We now have a Momma's boy on our hands.

The poor little guy was burning up. They told us that he had a cough, but when I put my lips to his forehead it was obvious that he had a fever, and he was on fire.

We brought him back to our room, where I continued to hold him and talk to him. The guys went to find a straw, since his update indicated that he likes straws and he wasn't keen on his sippy cup. That allowed the two of us to have some alone time to bond.

We found out his Chinese nickname is "Weifeng" (pronounced way-fung), so that is what we will call him until he's a little more comfortable. Jimmy ordered some room service, which Daniel refused to eat. Every time I offered food to him, he would turn away as if to say, "No thank you, I'm not staying!" Bless his little heart. It's been a tough day for him.

He's now sound asleep in our bed, and we will sleep with him tonight. We are concerned about his fever and his cold, so we feel it's best to keep him close. Let the bonding begin...

Gotcha Day

As I now read over that long-ago blog post, I realized even then that there was no room for fear. There was no room for error. Jimmy and I needed Daniel to realize right away how much we loved him, and that we would provide for him *instantly*. I did not want our son to be stressed out with the transition, especially given his physical condition, and I was equally concerned with his age and potential emotional baggage.

Since Daniel was almost two years old, we knew that some attachments had likely been formed with caretakers and his birth parents. With the knowledge that he was given up at seven months of age, we felt like our son had to have known love. The mere thought is heartbreaking, but in my mind, it indicates that his birth parents loved him and were probably devastated to give him up. I knew, with every cell of my being, that I needed to go into that conference room and be his loving mother *immediately*.

This was such a different experience than our union with Madi. I remember being so fearful, so nervous, having never mothered a child before. Motherhood was all new, uncharted territory to me then, and I was very insecure. In Daniel's case, I felt totally secure. I already knew that I was a good mommy. I already knew that I could love a child the minute he or she was placed into my arms. Madi was proof of that. As I watch the video footage now of our Gotcha Day with Daniel, I am so thankful to see comforting reassurance that I truly *was* his mother from the minute I first held Daniel in my arms. I loved him unconditionally.

The Orphanage Director then handed us a gift for our son – a Jade Buddha hand necklace believed to help cure disease. It is customary for adoptive parents to give gifts to the officials in China, and it was at that moment I realized that – in the excitement – we'd forgotten to bring our gifts for the Orphanage Director and Daniel's orphanage caregivers. Though our gifts were completely assembled and gift-bagged, we'd left them behind in the hotel room. Thankfully, Lisa reassured me that we'd have another chance.

I mentioned in my blog post that Daniel was sick when we took him. Jimmy and I were quite distraught when the Orphanage Director handed a feverish Daniel to us. As his eyes welled up with tears, he refused to make eye contact with any of us. It was obvious that Daniel was *very* sick. He was running a high fever, and we were very concerned about how this would affect a healthy child, never mind a child with a serious heart condition.

In Chinese, the Orphanage Director told our guide, "They should take him to see a doctor when they get him back home." She did not seem to treat Daniel's illness very seriously, and we were not at all satisfied with her suggestion. That was *two weeks away!* It made Jimmy and I wonder how long our baby had been sick. Our guide, Lisa, divulged that the last time she had visited the group home in the winter, Daniel seemed much more serious and withdrawn than he had last summer. This was obviously alarming news to both Jimmy and me.

Another contributing factor to our son's high temperature was the overkill of clothing he'd been dressed in. It is Chinese custom to bundle babies with multiple layers of clothing. When they gave him to us, Daniel was wearing two turtleneck shirts, a sweater, sweatpants, denim overalls, and an overcoat. Together, Jimmy and I managed to remove the coat and overalls without much resistance, but removing the first turtleneck sweater was nothing short of traumatic. Every time we tried to take it off he would cry, yet we knew it *had* to come off. He was shown wearing that same turtleneck in the photos that Holt had given us at our meeting in Beijing, so Lord knows how long he had been wearing it.

Lisa came over to him and spoke to him in Chinese to explain what we were doing and that we were trying to help him. As she lifted his arms, it literally took three of us to get that thing off of him. We fought with that shirt for a good ten seconds, which seemed like ten minutes, and the poor little guy was howling because it was stuck over his face and head. It was exhausting. Once we finally won the "wrestling match," it didn't take long to calm Daniel down, thank God. I rocked him back and forth, patting his chest and softly repeating, "It's okay…it's okay."

We washed and returned all of the other clothing to the orphanage, but that turtleneck was the one item of clothing we chose to keep – that pain in the you-know-what sweater labeled *JoJo* on the collar. Jimmy and I had planned to keep one article of clothing from Gotcha Day, and figured that sweater would certainly suffice. We would certainly never forget it! Now, we cherish it.

Grandpa Murphy, Jimmy, and I sat with Daniel in the conference room of the hotel for about half an hour, feeding him Cheerios with water and gaining his trust. We could see that Daniel wasn't sure how to drink from his sippy cup – it was obviously unfamiliar to him. We wasn't sure how to drink from his sippy cup – it was obviously unfamiliar to him. We did not want to leave that room until Jimmy and I were sure that Daniel felt more comfortable and realized that we were on *his* side. I held our son on my lap, while allowing him the freedom to take fistfuls of Cheerios from the container himself.

When we finally felt that Daniel was ready, the four of us ambled back up to our hotel rooms. The first thing we did was administer Motrin. The idea of giving Daniel medication was frightening, but Jimmy and I both knew that it would relieve his pain and make him comfortable.

When the guys slipped out to find some straws at the market, I slowly began to peel the remaining layers of clothing off of him. It was, however, really difficult because Daniel was so overtly attached to these articles of clothing. They were his security; all he'd had were the clothes on his back – no other possessions. I think for that reason, it terrified him that we were taking these items away from him, so I proceeded very cautiously (and slowly) through the course of the night. Eventually, once Daniel started to trust me, it became easier to remove the layers and by the end of the evening, he was bare-chested and wearing only his pajama bottoms. You could tell that Daniel wasn't used to having much access to his skin, because he would touch his chest and his belly as if he'd never known they were there.

Our son was also wearing a pair of little sneakers that must have been two sizes too small. We were never able to get them back on his feet after Jimmy removed them! Those ten little piggies were never so happy to breathe! I noticed that his little cupped toenails (a condition commonly found in children with Tetralogy of Fallot) were so long that they curled over the tops of his toes.

Since it was winter in China, and the orphanage kept the children tremendously bundled, they probably didn't bathe them much. We'd also heard that they probably kept Daniel more bundled than the other children in order to keep him from looking blue. The orphanage staff believed that if his temperature were kept warmer, then his cheeks would appear nice and rosy. Daniel's face appeared more than just "rosy." It actually looked quite red and blotchy. We weren't sure if that was because of his excessive clothing, or if his high fever and illness were to blame.

Once we had removed all those layers, it became easier to inspect our little one better. We could see that, from the shortness of his legs, Daniel's growth must have been stunted from the lack of oxygen flow through his body. We discovered a small patch of dark hair on Daniel's lower back, which can be common in children with Spina Bifida, though that was definitely not the cause in Daniel's case. That night, Jimmy and I also noticed that Daniel had patches of sores on his midriff and arms that he would pick at whenever he could get to them. We never did determine the cause. The poor little guy seemed to have so much stress pent up inside. We could see that we had our work cut out for us, but we also knew that everything was going to be just fine.

Our little warrior seemed to be very serious. He'd had a lot to be serious about, for sure. Those pictures we'd received at the orientation meeting a couple of days prior had given us fair warning. We had yet to see him smile, but we believed that the Good Lord had put him in the right family, and we were confident that once he got to know us better, Daniel would soon be smiling and laughing.

Initially, Daniel was not sure of Daddy or Grandpa Murphy, and he even cried when they came near him. I felt my husband's pain, but (thankfully) being the wonderful man that he is, Jimmy was wise enough to know that it was only temporary. He was so patient and such an awesome Dad that he allowed Daniel to bond on *his* terms, which willingly began that night when we were up with him at about 3:00 a.m.

Bonding with Daddy

Since he had passed on dinner, our baby boy was obviously very hungry and snacked on Cheerios and water. Jimmy took full advantage of the opportunity to meet his needs and gain his trust. During that bonding session, I responded to Daniel's hunger pangs by giving him his first dose of Juice Plus+® gummies, and I was ecstatic that he loved them instantly. As a passionate independent sales consultant for Juice Plus+® products, it truly thrilled me to get the added nutrition of 17 fruits, vegetables and grains into that little body, especially since his paperwork indicated that he was not fond of fruits or veggies at all. Thanks to the Motrin, Daniel no longer felt feverish, but he had been coughing throughout the night, so we decided that we should try to see a doctor very soon.

The next morning, our resourceful guide, Lisa, arranged for a pediatrician to come to our room and examine Daniel. And not just any pediatrician – for only twenty-five American dollars, the head doctor of the Children's Hospital in Nanchang made a house call to our hotel room! He was a fabulous doctor – very kind and gentle. Lisa translated for us, and we felt very much at ease despite the language barrier. It was clear that Daniel felt at ease, too. He was very relaxed and compliant with the pediatrician, and he seemed to comprehend that we were all trying to help him, not hurt him. The doctor immediately recognized the severity of Daniel's heart condition just by listening, and he urged us to have Daniel examined as soon as we returned to the United States. We assured him that appointments had already been set up and that a corrective plan was in place.

Daniel was quickly diagnosed with acute bronchitis. We'd brought along some antibiotics, and we had been in touch with our pediatric cardiologist via email. The cardiologist calculated the proper dosage, and we started to administer the medicine right away. The Chinese pediatrician also gave us an herbal liquid cough syrup to give him. Thankfully, Daniel was a real champ when it came to taking his medicine.

That evening, for the first time, we did a webcam call (via Skype) to Madi. Daniel was sleeping soundly, and Madi was quite agitated that she couldn't see him in action. She was devastated, actually. And when she wasn't able to communicate with Daniel, she threw herself back on her bed in a mound of exasperation. It was a pretty difficult situation for a four-and-a-half-year-old who expected instant gratification! We carried the laptop computer over to the bed and hovered over Daniel with the webcam so Madi could see him lying there. She needed to just see that *he was real,* and that he was finally ours. We explained to her that he was sick and promised to Skype again as soon as possible so she could talk to him.

It was clear to see, right away, that Daniel really was a good little boy, just as the Orphanage Director had told us on Gotcha Day. We watched him become a little more playful every day, and he quickly began to bond very well with all of us. We still had work to do on the smiling, though we were starting to see glimpses of that, too. Jimmy and I just couldn't wait to hear a good old-fashioned belly laugh come out of that baby.

Daniel was also a noticeably beautiful little boy. When I asked our guide, Lisa, what the Chinese culture considered as the "perfect" child, she described this perfect child as a male gender with fair, pale skin, big round black eyes, and cherry red lips. That *was* Daniel. She had just described our son! Unfortunately for Daniel, even though he *appeared* to be the "perfect" child by cultural standards, he was not simply because of his medical condition. And that would mean a lifetime of routine medical follow-up that his birth parent(s) probably just could not have afforded, or perhaps weren't equipped to deal with.

By the next day, Daniel was all about the boys. Jimmy and Grandpa are so much fun – I knew it was only a matter of time! At breakfast, Daniel started teasing Jimmy and me with a piece of bread. Not only did we get some smiles, but we also got a tiny bit of that much longed-for belly laugh! I looked across the table and saw tears in Grandpa Murphy's eyes. Actually, we all had tears in our eyes. We'd truly had no idea how long it would take Daniel to come out of his shell. In the back of our minds, we had all secretly feared that he might have been emotionally scarred from his past, or his transition, and it was such a tremendous relief to see that somewhere in there was a happy little person. All three of us were overcome with emotion.

Grandpa's boy

That same morning, our family took a bus trip to the Ministry of Civil Affairs, and Daniel legally became ours. Jimmy and I openly answered their questions about our intentions and promised the officials that we would love our son unconditionally and give him all the opportunities that he deserved in life. The Civil Affairs Officer then presented us with a beautiful carved piece of bamboo as a gift for Daniel. The three of us felt so proud to stand by the American flag and take pictures together with our little guy. It was an important day, and Jimmy and I were so thankful that the Lord had delivered Daniel into our family.

By day three with our son, it was clear that the antibiotics were working. His skin was beginning to look less blotchy and red, as it had before, and his cough was improving a little each day. Additionally, we had finally been able to Skype with Madi while Daniel was awake. The best time was between 7:00 – 7:30 a.m. in Florida, which was 8:00 – 8:30 in the evening where we were in China. Madi was so fascinated by Daniel's every move, but he wasn't so sure about her.

Since the webcam was a new and unfamiliar experience for him, he focused his attention on playing with Grandpa Murphy, while Madi would watch them laugh and play. She was so excited that Daniel was finally with us, and she could hardly wait to get her hands on him. Since Daniel had ignored her sweet nothings on Skype, Madi decided to send her new little brother his first email:

Hi Daniel,

I love you, Daniel. I'm going to make you laugh. Let's do knock-knock jokes. I hope you have a great trip when you go to the airport. I love you, Daniel. I went to the mall to play. I had ice cream there. I have three pairs of new shoes. The school liked my mushrooms. My Hello Kitty shoes broke at school. Now send it.

Chapter Six

THE FIRST DAYS

The city of Nanchang, reported to have a population of 5,042,865 at the 2010 Census, didn't, in our opinion, have the feel of such a "big city." But we soon discovered (since we had to keep our hotel window open out of necessity for cool air) that it was absolutely the noisiest city we had ever been in. Car horns honked – literally – all night long. And the sounds of traffic and industrial commotion never seemed to wane.

We woke up every single morning to the sound of firecrackers in the very early hours. We were told that these explosives are typically used on two occasions in China – weddings and funerals, and that the morning occurrences were likely for a funeral. Along with the noise intrusion came massive amounts of air pollution. Honestly, there were times during our visit that we found it difficult to breathe in that city because of the fumes.

On January 26th, two days after being united with Daniel, our guide recognized a little girl in our hotel from the same group home in Daniel's orphanage. Her adoptive family, who resides in Spain, happened to be staying in the same hotel where we were, and it turned out that Daniel and this sweet little girl had shared a bed together! What are the chances? Her adoptive family named her Clara, and when she spotted Daniel, she was so excited that she pointed him out to her new brother and even tried to "mother" him a little bit. Daniel's reaction was curious. It was clear that he recognized Clara, but he appeared to be confused by their reunion, presumably because he and Clara were not at the orphanage where he was used to seeing her on a regular basis.

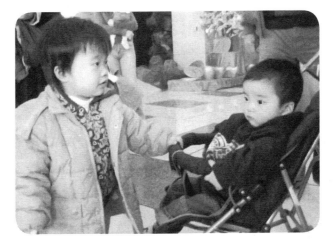

Daniel (on right) with Clara

Shortly after Daniel's reunion with Clara, our family boarded the tour bus to go to a local park, and Daniel – who looked a bit sad – promptly fell sound asleep on Grandpa's lap. We suspected that Daniel was quietly grieving, and it was interesting to us that he seemed to grieve much like Madi had. Neither one of them cried – they just coped by turning the world off and going to sleep.

When we arrived at our destination, Daniel woke up and made it clear that he did not want to get off the bus. He clung to Grandpa like Velcro and fought to stay on board. Did he think was going back to the orphanage? Jimmy and I wondered what was happening in that little, vulnerable mind. When I really think about these children – these orphans and their courage – I believe they are some of the bravest people in the world. Literally uprooted from all that they know and about to face an entirely new life, they stoically accept all the change that awaits them (though the bonding process varies). The openness of their hearts is astonishing to me. We knew that Daniel's insecure moments were golden opportunities to show him that he was *with us now*, and he wouldn't be going anywhere without us.

That same evening at dinner, Jimmy and I finally got what we had been waiting for – the "whole enchilada" – a smile, a belly laugh, and a spunky, happy little two-year-old boy. Granted, it involved throwing chopsticks across the table, but we didn't care! We discovered that Daniel had the cutest dimples, which we hadn't even known about!

Daniel truly was a different child that night. Perhaps he was starting to understand that he was staying with us. Maybe seeing Clara that morning – and seeing that she also had a new family – mentally solidified his status with our family. Our son teased and played at the table; he had a hearty appetite, and even fed himself a bowl of noodles. Jimmy and I felt like we were finally getting somewhere with Daniel. As his true colors began to emerge, my husband and I also started to realize that this adorable little boy was going to keep us very, very busy!

The first smiles

The next morning, we received another email message from Daniel's big sister:

Dear Mommy and Daddy,

I love you. I hope you have a great trip home. I love Daniel. I gave Bubba a great makeover. I got a brush for picture day at First United Methodist School. I got a brush, and when you open it, it is a comb. I love you Mommy and Daddy. I love Daniel, too. I love Grandpa Murphy, too. I got M&Ms at school today at Banyan Creek. The cats all missing you. Grandpa and Bubba feed me junk food. They give me lots of salami. I'm been poopin' good. We are going to the Library to return the books and movies, and we're going to get some movies and books. Now send it.

January 28th was my 43rd birthday, and the only thing missing from our celebration was Madi. Daniel was now on the mend, and he was becoming a tiny tornado! Jimmy and I were so thankful to see his bubbly, spicy side flourish! We enjoyed a relaxed morning with a slow pace, and Daniel was all smiles and giggles as the four of us played together in the hotel room.

Daniel was totally enamored with Jimmy's black rubber wristwatch, which he'd borrowed from Grandpa Wharton for the trip. Jimmy began to let Daniel wear it whenever he expressed an interest, and Daniel loved that watch so much that Grandpa ended up giving it to him after we returned home.

Daniel wearing Grandpa's watch

We quickly realized that we needed to start baby-proofing everything. It was time to, once again, be more careful about where we set things that were within baby's reach. I was busy doing something (probably typing on the computer) and turned around to see Daniel holding a Tsing Tao beer can in his hands. It was evident that he had taken a sip (the can – thank goodness – was practically empty) and had spilled beer all down his bare belly! He looked so cute, although I gave the guys a heap of grief for leaving open beer cans within reach of the baby!

Later that morning, we decided to venture out to the nearby pedestrian street (these streets are strictly for walking – no cars allowed) for shopping. Daniel desperately needed a pair of good shoes that properly fit, and we had been carrying him around in Robeez slippers that were about two sizes too big. It had been customary for Grandma Pauline to buy each grandchild their first pair of shoes, but since she wasn't there with us, Grandpa Murphy generously carried on the tradition.

We saw Clara again down in the hotel lobby that afternoon, and this time their reunion was more joyful as they tossed balloons around together. But as soon as we left the hotel, Daniel's serious side came out again. It was becoming painfully obvious that he didn't like leaving the hotel perhaps out of fear that he would be leaving us for another change. We were now able to read him pretty well, and we were wise to his behavior pattern. Jimmy and I realized, again, that these were simply more perfect opportunities to reinforce the truth that he would be staying with us. Daniel was notably attached to Daddy that day, so I began to take the back seat. I was totally okay with that because I knew that Daniel would get lots of face time with Mommy back at home.

Our guide, Lisa, took us to another fabulous local restaurant that night where we celebrated my birthday. Lisa surprised me with a beautiful birthday cake, and we enjoyed a lovely evening out. The food in Nanchang was incredible, which was a refreshing change from our trip to bring Madi home. In Gansu province, we had been part of a large group of eleven families, so all of the pre-planned meal outings had to be arranged at restaurants that could accommodate our large group. The restaurants tended to be more "touristy," and the food just wasn't great. This time around however, we were one of only three families in our group that adopted children from Nanchang. One of the families had adopted twin baby girls, so it wasn't so easy for them to leave the hotel, since they were very busy adjusting to their new double-duty parental status.

That left us with just one other family, which meant we could go practically anywhere we wanted to. We really enjoyed spending time with the other couple, Allison and Chris, who adopted a beautiful healthy infant girl named Zoe. They had waited over five years for their precious bundle. We were thankful that they had similar expectations, and we seemed to be on the same wavelength when it came to dining and various outings in the province. Our guide, Lisa, having grown up in Nanchang, knew all the right spots. We ate some really superb authentic food this time around and enjoyed a great local experience, but we were ready to leave Nanchang.

Nanchung airport with our guide, Lisa

We'd had a memorable stay, but Jimmy and I had accomplished everything we needed to in Jiangxi province, and we definitely felt prepared to move on. Now – officially – we had our baby boy. We just wanted to do what was necessary to get Daniel home to meet Madi and everyone else who was anxiously awaiting his arrival.

Chapter Seven

BONDING IN GUANGZHOU

It was such a relief to be at the final phase of our trip, and Daniel seemed to handle the travel to Guangzhou quite well, though he was pretty restless in bed that evening after we'd arrived to yet another new and unfamiliar place. The next morning, with little sleep, posted about the beginning of our homestretch.

GOODBYE NANCHANG, HELLO PARADISE! | Jan. 29, 2010

Last night, we arrived in paradise, and we are so relieved to be here! We didn't realize just how antsy and "Nanchang-ed out" we'd felt until we arrived at the White Swan Hotel! Guangzhou is a coastal city with a tropical climate, much like Florida's. This is great for us, since Daniel's body can acclimate to our weather before we even leave China. And, the American Consulate is located here, so every adoptive family from the U.S. ends their trip in Guangzhou.

The White Swan Hotel is really well prepared for adoptive families, and it is truly an inspirational sight as we look around. There are literally hundreds of American families, most of whom have adopted special needs children to extend their biological families. Some have five, six, seven children – some biological, some adopted, some healthy, some with medical conditions. It is a humbling experience. As a society, America has truly responded to the call to find families for these beautiful and special children despite their medical conditions.

Daniel handled his first airline flight beautifully. He never really fussed, but his eyes were big as saucers as we trekked through the airport and got on the plane. He was thrilled with the big lollipop we brought him to distract him from the turbulence. Last night, we walked next door to Lucy's Bar & Grill, and a cheeseburger with fries never tasted so good! The night's sleep was bumpy, because Daniel had trouble settling in and whimpered throughout the night. He was in a twin size bed with Mommy, so maybe space was an issue, but I'm sure he was simply over-stimulated by the change of scenery, and the fact that he'd been introduced to more unfamiliar surroundings. We will be here for a week for our visa processing, so it should be a nice transition for him. Daniel is being exposed to more and more American faces with Chinese children.

This morning we went to the local medical clinic where all the children over age two had to have the TB tests that are required by the U.S. government. Grandpa Murphy held Daniel while we consoled him. But it's never fun getting shots, is it? The U.S. also requires immunizations, which we must face on Monday. Some of the families who arrived in Guangzhou earlier took their children for immunizations yesterday, and some of the kids needed up to seven shots. We are not looking forward to that, and hope for fewer injections...

The White Swan Hotel, on Shamian Island in Guangzhou, is such a breath of fresh air for American travelers with adoptive children. It is a luxurious five-star hotel with waterfalls, koi ponds, a

"Western" breakfast buffet beyond compare, and a well-stocked playroom – sponsored by Mattel – for the children. At the time, every adoptive family who stayed there, as a gift, received a brand new collectible Barbie doll. The "American" Barbie doll has long blond hair, and holds an adopted Chinese baby girl!

Shamian Island is a seemingly safe place, loaded with a variety of restaurants and souvenir shops selling everything from authentic Chinese clothing, to tea, jewelry, jade, musical instruments, paintings, fans, and truly any Chinese souvenir one could think of.

That is where we met Jordan, a kind Christian shopkeeper who named Daniel our "Lucky Link." As he scribed our son's new name, *Daniel James*, in Chinese characters, he wrote "Lucky" next to Daniel and "Link" next to James. At the time, Jimmy and I wondered what the translation meant – a link to what? We remarked that perhaps Daniel was our link to Grandma Pauline. Jimmy and I were both quite intrigued.

There are several outdoor parks on the island, which include painted metal fitness equipment. These parks are quite different from our American parks, which are mostly geared towards children. The fitness equipment in China is suitable for all ages – much like an outdoor gym. It is very common for locals, adults and children, to come to these parks together for their exercise. There are various bronze statues scattered around the island that depict life as it was during earlier periods on the island as well as some from more recent times. There was one statue, in particular, that resonated with us. It was a bronze sculpture of a well-rounded, older woman, and we lovingly remarked that it reminded us of Grandma Pauline.

After the relatively sleepless night that I posted about, we ended up having a phenomenal day with Daniel. It was Sunday, and with our group we attended a non-denominational church service at Christ

Church Shamian, the Island's British Protestant church that was built in 1865. Though the service ran a bit long for an over-tired two-year-old, it was indeed beautiful. The choir was heavenly, and they sang in English, which surprised us. We recognized our language, though we could barely understand the words except for a slow and melodic chorus of "Hallelujah," which was crystal clear. Grandpa Murphy swore that he saw Grandma Pauline as an angel at Christ Church in Guangzhou that day. It was no surprise that she was there with us on our journey.

Inside Our Lady of Lourdes

After the service, we decided to seek out Our Lady of Lourdes, the French Catholic Church on the Island. This quaint structure, which has been restored and stands on the main boulevard, was completed in 1892. When we arrived at the church, within walking distance, Mass was already over and the sanctuary doors were locked. Inquisitive me wandered around the perimeter of the church and found an elderly Chinese woman, who appeared to be the "gatekeeper." When I asked if we could go inside, she escorted

Jimmy and me to the front entry, opened the church's front door with a large key and kindly instructed us (in Chinese) to close the door when we were through! It was an amazing experience. Jimmy and I went inside that small, quaint sanctuary, took in our peaceful surroundings, and spent some time to praise the Lord.

There was something so serene about being inside that church, alone together, with Jesus. There was such an intimate, holy feeling that overcame us and gave us both the most tremendous sense of comfort. I loved that my husband and I were a world away from home, yet we were still *home*. We locked up when we were done, as instructed, and went on our way. In the courtyard outside, Jimmy and I were relieved to find that Daniel had fallen asleep in his stroller while he waited with Grandpa Murphy. For the past few days, our son had been protesting his nap once he'd discovered that life was just too much fun for sleeping!

That afternoon, we opted to take a bus with the Holt group to the jade and pearl markets for a shopping excursion. We had been reunited with our entire Holt group from Beijing, so there were many families on board the tour bus getting reacquainted. Daniel, who was a bit overwhelmed with the larger group dynamic, stuck to Grandpa Murphy and Daddy like glue.

Jimmy and I half-heartedly shopped for jade and pearls, but ended up buying nothing. We honestly had everything we needed with Daniel in our arms. We knew that, on this trip, we wouldn't be shopping for much. It just wasn't on our agenda (or in our budget) this time around. While we strolled through the market, a kind shopkeeper began conversing with Daniel in Chinese and pulled out a large piece of hard candy for him. Before Jimmy and I even had time to react, she popped it into his mouth! As we walked away, with a reasonable amount of concern, I begged, "Jimmy – please get that out of his mouth before he chokes!" Daniel must have known what I'd said because he closed his lips so tightly that I don't think we'd have been able to pry them open no matter how hard we tried!

Getting to know Daniel and watching his personality slowly emerge was a wonderful adventure every day. At one point during our shopping trip, he watched Jimmy put his sunglasses on his head, and Daniel totally imitated him by then propping the sunglasses crookedly on his own little head. And he did a pretty good job too!

Our family had grown close to several of the other adoptive families in our group, and that night, we went to the local Italian restaurant for dinner with some of them. Of course, my little buddy, Jaeden (who reminded me so much of Madi), and her family were among the group. After enjoying so much authentic Chinese food on our trip, Italian cuisine was a welcome change. Don't get me wrong – the authentic food in China is delicious, but after a while, we just longed for a change! It was Daniel's first time to eat non-Chinese noodles (that we knew of), and he loved slurping his buttered spaghetti. Daniel had behaved so well in all of the restaurants, including this one. He seemed to embrace every experience and clearly enjoyed the quality time with his new family and the larger group that joined us.

Daniel enjoying spaghetti

The four of us also enjoyed the big daily breakfast buffet at the White Swan, where we soon discovered Daniel's passion for yogurt. Jimmy and I had heard that yogurt was probably not something fed to the orphanage children due to its need for unavailable refrigeration. The hotel offered an unlimited amount of drinkable yogurts in a variety of flavors that we would pop a straw into, and Daniel would empty them in seconds flat. He seemed to be making up for lost time and began to consume *at least* two of those every morning. We would sneak one or two in the diaper bag to keep in our room for him, too. We could quickly see that yogurt was destined to become a favorite staple in his diet.

On February 1st, our group had bright and early appointments at the medical clinic for the children's medical exams. These are required by the U.S. government in order for the children to obtain their visas. Having been through it before with Madi, we were familiar with the exhausting process. They move you to and from three stations that handle different phases of the medical exam. At the first station, they took vitals, and Daniel (with his clothes and shoes on) weighed in at 27 pounds. The second station focused on development, and the medical examiner tested Daniel's vision and hearing. Their testing methods were pretty basic. They actually used a rubber squeaky toy for the hearing evaluation! The last station was our major concern – Daniel's medical evaluation and vaccine analysis. We anxiously waited until the full exam was over to hear the sinking news that he had no immunization records from his orphanage, so Daniel needed all seven vaccines. Jimmy and I dreaded hearing this, and it was pretty scary news for all of us to take in.

Three different doctors approached Jimmy and me and asked questions about Daniel's current condition in order to make sure that his heart could handle the stress of the vaccines. We could clearly see – from their body language – that they were nervous, which made us quite uncomfortable. Unfortunately, Jimmy and I knew that if Daniel weren't able to take the shots, our government would not grant him a visa; therefore, there wasn't an option. The group of doctors thoroughly reviewed Daniel's medical records, which was reassuring, and then they finally decided to proceed with the vaccinations.

We had friends in our group who vowed that this process would be lobbied against in the very near future. It seemed so wrong to endanger any of these children. We were thrilled to find out that this protocol has since been changed, and an exemption may now be granted by filing an affidavit stating that immunizations will be given in the U.S. within a specific timeframe from the adopted child's arrival home.

Everyone else in our group was done with their exams and had gone from the medical clinic, while we still waited anxiously for our son's vaccinations. Daniel was just beginning to really trust us, and here we had to subject him to this torture. When it was time, Jimmy and I asked Grandpa Murphy to hold Daniel while we tried our best to console our son. Those sixty seconds were sheer agony for all of us. It was one of many painful experiences that our sweet son would endure. All four of us were sweating profusely. Almost immediately afterwards, Daniel passed out on Daddy's shoulder from the stress, exhaustion, and pain of the shots. We thanked God when it was finally over.

Daniel after his medical exam in Guangzhou

After a good nap and some Motrin to relieve the pain, we took Daniel to the second floor of the White Swan for his traditional "Red Couch photo" with our Holt group. It is tradition for adopted Chinese children to have a group photo taken together. All the kids (or at least those who will comply) are dressed in traditional Chinese outfits and situated on a red velvet couch. We were a few minutes late to the group photo, and some of the children had already been plucked from the couch because they were so visibly upset. Daniel ended up behind the couch, on Jimmy's shoulders, for the group photo. I was just thankful that he wasn't crying, especially given the earlier events of the day!

Daniel looked like such a tough little warrior in his cherry-red silk suit with its golden dragon emblazoned across the front. He seemed to have a different gleam in his eye when he wore that traditional Chinese outfit. By then, he had already gotten wise to his paparazzi mother. Every time I tried to take his picture, he knew the precise second that my camera would beep, and he would turn his face away just as the picture would snap! I must have taken ten pictures of the back of the little stinker's head that night.

Little Warrior

HAPPY BIRTHDAY, DANIEL! | February 2, 2010

Daniel had a very special birthday today, especially for his parents. It meant so much to us that we were able to spend his 2nd birthday as a family. His day started with a Skype birthday call from sister Madi. We can see that he's becoming more familiar with her since we've been Skyping. Modern technology – what a blessing!

We spent our day going to the safari park (zoo). It was Daniel's first trip to the zoo, and you could see on his face that he was fascinated with the animals. There was one point when Daddy took Daniel to feed the giraffes, and the poor little guy just freaked out. He was terrified to be that up close and personal! We saw about twenty live pandas, and koala bears, too. On the way back to the hotel, Daniel fell asleep on Grandpa Murphy's lap.

We went back to the Italian restaurant tonight for dinner with all the Holt families. We sang Happy Birthday to Daniel several times and he loved it. Apparently, the tune is the same in Chinese, and it was obvious to everyone (from the smile on his face) that he had heard it before. Tomorrow is our oath-taking ceremony at the U.S. Consulate. Only a few more days, and we'll be home; it seems like we've been gone for months. We cannot wait to get home and be reunited with our gorgeous little girl. We miss her so much.

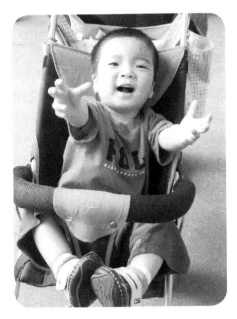

Birthday at the Safari Park

Afraid of giraffes!

On February 3rd, we had our children's oath and swearing in ceremony at the U.S. Consulate, which was an enormously moving occasion, to say the least. As the Consulate Officer announced all of the birthdays for the month, our Daniel Murphy was the first child mentioned. She made note of how many special needs families were in the room, and announced that it was a record-breaking year for special needs adoptions. The Officer also brought special recognition to a family who was back in China for their ninth adoption!

I mentioned special needs adoptions earlier in a blog post, and I need to elaborate because I think that is one of the things that impacted me the most on our trip. It's amazing how drastically the adoption picture has changed in China over the past several years. When we adopted Madi, the White Swan Hotel was swimming with healthy infant girls.

It was so different this time around, because healthy infants were the *minority*. And, there were many more boys this time. Some were healthy, but most had medical conditions. Some were younger and some older. But each was so beautiful in his or her own way. The special needs that we noticed included: cleft lip, cleft palate, heart conditions, cerebral palsy, spina bifida, hydrocephalus, blindness, hearing issues, birthmarks, orthopedic issues such as club foot, and various limb differences. In the Chinese culture, these children are commonly seen as flawed, but the Americans who choose to adopt them (and people from many other countries, as well) still see these children as pure perfection and do not allow their conditions and differences to define who they are. It was such a strong and beautiful statement about *our* culture and *our* beliefs. Jimmy and I couldn't have been prouder to be American, and we couldn't wait to be back in the land of the free and the home of the brave.

It wasn't until after we'd returned home that my father said to me, "Lisa, you should read what your brother wrote on the blog." I couldn't imagine what Andrew could have written that touched my family so, or what emotions would come over me when my eyes met his heartfelt and endearing words. I love my brother, Andrew, who has a true gift – for sure – and a heart of pure gold.

TURNING IN MY KEYS | February 5, 2010

I am now ready to give the keys to this blog back to its owner, as they are coming home with Daniel now. I cannot begin to explain how happy and honored I was to be your humble narrator on this journey that my sister and her family had embarked upon. It was a point of immense pride that I was the first person to see these blog entries as they were sent from China. That I got to email with Lisa several times a day, not just on blog entries, but other, more trivial issues, kept me in touch with their adventure in a way that I enjoyed. It wasn't work...

I know that this blog will be kept to show Madi and Daniel their origins and the outpouring of love during these times. Blogs are the new photo album. Lisa, Jimmy, Madi and Daniel are now going to the next chapter in their life, and we'll all be watching. And now, a small note on disintermediation. Or, "How can a regional superpower and information blocker as big as China be completely thwarted by a mildly determined blogger and her somewhat wired brother?" China's Great (Fire) Wall of China was put into place to disable the sharing of unwanted information. In that, it is a complete failure.

Whether I was in New Hampshire, Burlington, Boston, Frankfurt or Helsinki, I would open my laptop periodically and approve comments or move a blog post from email to blogger. At one point, I approved a bunch of comments using my cell phone from an Indian restaurant in downtown Helsinki in a blizzard. Billions of yuan and hundreds of thousands of Chinese security people were sidestepped without a serious thought.

That should be a lesson to those petty tyrants who would try to stifle the free-flow of information. China's awesome power was completely steamrolled by a power that they still fail to comprehend: the love of a family that travels halfway around the world to find their son, the love of their family to help spread the word, the love of their friends who thirst for the slightest scrap of information. And — above all — the love of God to bless us for all of this to happen. I will now sign off, knowing that this blog is back in the right hands. Godspeed. Now send it.

– Andrew

♡

Chapter Eight

HOME

$\mathcal{T}$o say that the trip home from China was "chaotic" would be an understatement. On the morning of our departure from Guangzhou, we first boarded a bus and headed for the American Embassy to pick up our visas. They must have been behind schedule, because we waited a solid hour for the visas to be collected and then distributed to the families. The children in our group were already getting quite restless in the lobby, and this was just the beginning of the day's travel!

Once the visas were finally ready, the bus then delivered us to the train station where we waited another two hours and finally boarded a train to Hong Kong. We had been so excited for our first train ride experience in China, but it turned out that we really didn't get to see much scenery. The guys were just thankful for the ice cold draft beer that was served. We arrived in Hong Kong at approximately 10:00 p.m. Most of the children were asleep by that time, with an occasional outburst of tears here and there.

We exited the train station, gathered our bags, and looked for our bus to the hotel. This was the longest day of travel we had experienced thus far, and the entire group appeared to be wiped out. The tour guide on the bus must not have had children because it was 10:30 p.m., the overhead lights were on, and she was practically screaming into the microphone with excitement about Hong Kong and all its attractions. This was clearly not the right time, and this was definitely not the right audience! Everyone on the bus was quite annoyed and attempted to "shush" her several times. The poor girl just didn't get it, though we did finally persuade her to dim the overhead lights. We suffered through her enthusiastic tour guide narrative and finally made it to our hotel.

At this point, it was very late (almost midnight) and we were starving, so the guys went downstairs to order a couple of sandwiches and french fries from the hotel bar/restaurant. Our "midnight snack" cost almost one hundred dollars! We had been warned about the prices in Hong Kong, but we had no idea! Daniel was sound asleep, and we knew the next day would be another long day of travel, so the three of us collapsed with sweet dreams of finally being home again.

The next morning, we rose very early and hurried down to the lobby for checkout. Our group had stayed at the airport hotel, so we only needed to walk through a breezeway to enter the airport. Thankfully, check in was uneventful, and we made our way over to the fast food court for breakfast. All of us were actually thrilled to see a food court!

The flight from Hong Kong to Newark was simply disastrous. We were "that family" that everyone else wishes weren't on the plane! Daniel barely slept, and cried for almost the entire fourteen-hour flight. He just could not get comfortable, bless his heart. In hindsight, our son was probably suffering from the ear infection that he would soon be diagnosed with at home, but he was also just plain exhausted (and perhaps confused). At this point, Daniel wanted absolutely nothing to do with Mama. All that bonding with Daddy and Grandpa Murphy in China – well, those were the only two people he wanted to see in front of him now, especially Grandpa Murphy.

I felt sad and guilty that I wasn't able to console my son. He would barely allow me to hold him without pitching himself out of my arms and into his Grandpa's. It was painful for me, especially since I knew that it was a lot of added physical stress on Grandpa

Murphy. As much as he wanted to be there for his grandson, he was just wiped out from the trip. I forgot to mention that both my poor husband and father-in-law were sick with stomach bugs from their midnight snack in Hong Kong. Suffice it to say, it wasn't the best hundred dollars we'd spent on our trip. Jimmy barely had time to make it out of the bathroom, before Daniel was loudly demanding to be held in his arms.

We were fortunate to make our connection from Newark, New Jersey to West Palm Beach, Florida, though it was an *extremely* close call. We had only a two-hour window to get through customs, immigration, baggage claim, baggage re-check, security clearance, and then to, literally, run to our gate. The clear highlight of our scurry was the fact that, since Jimmy and I had both traveled to bring him home, Daniel became an American citizen the moment those little feet stepped on U.S. soil. I had déjà vu from our trip home with Madi in September of 2006. On that occasion, we failed to make our scheduled connecting flight. This time, thank God, we did.

At one point, Grandpa – who was so stressed out and frazzled by my irrational behavior under travel duress – left his suitcase right in the middle of the airport at a security threshold! It was sheer insanity, and poor Daniel felt the tension, too. He was crying loudly as we ran through the airport desperately trying to find our gate, which (by the way) had been moved clear across the airport.

With merely minutes left before the gate closed, we realized that neither we – nor Daniel – had eaten a thing in hours. Jimmy saved the day and sprinted to the nearest kiosk to purchase a few bananas and a couple of bottles of water, and by the grace of God, we finally made it on the plane with virtually seconds to spare. We staggered back to our seats, which were located in the last two rows of the airplane.

The stress of it all had just been too much for me. I had a weak moment and broke down in tears. I literally lost it. Jimmy, being the "rock" that he always is, did his best to console me. It wasn't supposed to happen this way. I was so gutturally fearful that Daniel wouldn't make it through another flight. I couldn't imagine how his exhausted little body could tolerate much more crying or much more stress. I was so scared that his heart couldn't take it and that the whole situation had simply been too much for him.

Once again, the only person who seemed able to soothe our son was Grandpa Murphy. He held Daniel during the entire three-hour flight from Newark to West Palm Beach, so our exhausted baby could get some desperately needed sleep. I was a nervous wreck because Grandpa kept nodding off with Daniel in his arms, and I thought for sure that the two of them were going to hit the floor! Jimmy was able to keep me grounded and calm, and even made me laugh a few times. My husband's ability to lighten 'heavy' situations is one of the many things that I love about him.

Obviously, Grandpa was a Godsend, and I honestly don't know how we could have made the trip without his help. This was almost the end of our journey, and it was really hitting him hard that Grandma Pauline wasn't there with him. In spirit, however, we all know that she had been with us the whole time.

When we arrived at the airport, we were greeted by the most beautiful sight for sore eyes – our beautiful daughter, Madi, and Bubba too. It was like finding the pot of gold at the end of the rainbow. Jimmy and I fell to our knees to hug, hold and kiss her. It seemed as if we had been away from her for a year, and she seemed to have grown *so much* in just two weeks.

Madi obviously loved seeing us, but she was more excited to meet Daniel. She approached him so cautiously and tenderly, obviously remembering how shy he had been on Skype. She was instantly the perfect big sister. Jimmy and I were so relieved to be back at home – tears of joy streamed down both of our faces. Our mission had finally been accomplished, and we were a family of four.

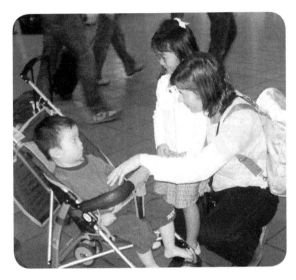

Madi meets Daniel at the airport

Our first hurdle heading home was the car seat. Daniel had been through enough, and he clearly wasn't in the mood to be introduced to an isolated seat with major restraints. It was not the night for a fight – at least that's how we felt about it, so Grandpa Murphy held Daniel the whole ride home. We took our chances, but Daniel was comfortable, and he certainly deserved to be. As she stared adoringly at her little brother in the back seat of the van, Madi was completely mesmerized. Jimmy and I were just so relieved that we were all together.

When we arrived at our house, we were surprised by a small gathering of close friends to welcome us back. Grandpa was anxiously awaiting our arrival, and Sherril and her husband, Matt, were at our house with their kids, Jonathon and Julianna. They were accompanied by Aunt Lori and Uncle Blake – Sherril's relatives whom we'd claimed as our own. Our friends Lisa and Mike were there with their daughters, Carmelina and Sophia, two of Madi's closest friends (who are also adopted from China).

At first, Jimmy and I were afraid that Daniel would be overwhelmed, but he handled the situation beautifully. He loved seeing children, and it seemed as though our son knew we were home. Fortunately, the kids all made sure that they didn't crowd him too much. It was difficult for Madi to give Daniel the space he needed, but she did a great job, given the excitement of her little brother finally coming home. The festivities were short-lived, as everyone respected the fact that Daniel needed a chance to breathe as well as take in his new surroundings calmly and quietly. He was exhausted.

Smitten

In Daniel's bedroom, we had placed both a full-size bed and a crib, since Jimmy and I weren't sure which he would prefer. We gave him the choice and he clearly had – based on his body language – decided on the bed. That was fine with us, since we wanted Daniel to feel totally comfortable in his new home, so we surrounded him with pillows to keep him from rolling off the bed. We were soon given – through the goodness of friends – a set of bed rails for our son's protection.

The next morning when they woke, Jimmy and I brought Daniel and Madi into our bed to snuggle and watch cartoons together. It was painfully obvious that Daniel wasn't pleased about sharing our attention with another child, but after they found a common love of teasing Mommy with Cheerios, the two began to bond instantly. They took turns teasing me and giggled with delight as they stuffed the cereal into their own mouths and not mine. Evidently, youthful mischief is universal. We introduced Daniel to his backyard and to the swing set that would become one of his favorite things. Our little monkey took to climbing the stairs of the play structure right away, and Jimmy and I could see that we would need to watch Daniel very closely, since he was obviously an accident waiting to happen.

STAY TUNED... | February 9, 2010

I have been severely hit by jet lag, not to mention a nasty sore throat. Our journey home was stressful beyond words, but the important thing is that *we are home*, and we are finally a family of four. I promise to post pictures and bring everyone up to date once I catch my breath, so please stay tuned...

The next week was a rough one. Poor little Daniel was diagnosed with a double ear infection (which explained his inconsolable behavior on the airplane), and he had a really tough time settling into both our time zone and his new surroundings. The week brought other hurdles, too. Daniel was less than thrilled with his high chair, and he was still terrified to take a bath. Jimmy and I soon managed to acclimate Daniel to both his car seat and his high chair, but he continued to have a *big* problem with the bathtub. And sleeping through the night was yet another story.

The week was frustrating for my husband and me, as well as for our son. Daniel cried in his sleep frequently, sometimes kicking and flailing to the point that we would have to wake him up to snap him out of it. Jimmy and I worked through it day by day, feeding him snacks in the middle of the night since his belly was still on China time. We had learned that the orphanage would wake him at 10:00 p.m. every night to go potty. Jimmy and I decided to try this one night, and it was nothing short of a disaster. So we figured out that they say "never wake a sleeping baby" for a good reason!

Daniel's schedule began to progressively transition. He continued to wake up crying, but he had only been home with us for one week. Daniel was still inseparable from my Jimmy, and he longed to be held by him any chance he could get. In fact, now that she was sharing Daddy's affection with a little brother, Madi was the same way. This was tough on Jimmy, because he worked from home. We quickly discovered that he would need to leave the house more often just so he could get his work done. It was confusing to Daniel when Daddy was at home but couldn't play with him during business hours, so I tried my best to keep the kids occupied with other things.

Daniel would refer to both of us as "*Mama.*" In fact, he would call anyone who looked nurturing "*Mama.*" It had been a big adjustment for Jimmy and me – as for millions of families before us – to grow our family from one to two kids, but we realized that it would get a little easier every day, especially as Daniel's comfort level grew, and we settled into our "new normal."

In the beginning, I constantly questioned my parenting abilities and wondered if it was more difficult to bring a two-year-old home rather than an infant. And, of course, the language barrier added an extra layer to the adjustment, as well. In my heart, I knew that Daniel carried a 'loyalty' to the nannies who had cared for him in China and that our bonding would be slow. But I was also aware that our connection would ultimately be stronger because of that slow and steady trust-building. I carried a lot of guilt about the fact that we were unable to give Madi the undivided attention she had become accustomed to pre-Daniel. I often joked to Madi that some families manage to care for ten kids, while I seemed to struggle with caring for just two!

During that time in which our daily activities were muddled from exhaustion, we were especially grateful for the kindness and generosity of others. Sherril made several grocery runs to Publix for us during our first week home. And our Mom's Club members and close friends delivered meals to us every other day for several weeks, which was such a Godsend – especially given Daniel's rough transition. It allowed us to maximize our time together without worrying about preparing dinner, which is generally a stretch for me under normal circumstances!

There was one mom, in particular, who went so above and beyond that it floored us. Sunny arrived at our doorstep with a five-course Chinese meal, which she'd made from scratch. She had actually researched foods from Daniel's province, and traveled to a nearby town to purchase groceries from an authentic Chinese market. Sunny had followed our family's journey through the blog, and she was smitten with Daniel. She wanted nothing more than for him to feel at home in his new surroundings, so she had poured her heart and soul into preparing that delicious meal to give Daniel a taste of his homeland.

Madi adored her little brother right out of the gate. It was heartwarming to see how gentle and patient she was, especially at her young age. Madi was such a loving sister, and really tried to be extra kind to Daniel. I can't say that there was no sibling rivalry, but it was minimal and completely within normal bounds. I think the toughest part was probably when Daniel didn't understand Madi's intentions.

Madi was constantly trying to mother and pamper Daniel, but he would sometimes mistake her acts of protection as acts of restriction! Since he couldn't successfully communicate with her verbally, Daniel would retaliate physically by pinching her or squeezing her forearm. He actually bit her one time, too. Madi would inevitably cry, more because her feelings were hurt from Daniel's acts of frustration than from pain. Then, of course, Daniel would break out in tears over the whole situation, and I'd have to calm them both down. Laughing always seemed to diffuse the situation – sorry but (sadly) sometimes that's my normal reaction to chaos at inappropriate times. Madi and Daniel were typical siblings! Despite these occasional flare-ups, she was always a huge help to us and to her little brother. He adored her, too.

In the very beginning, our son was a child of few words. It didn't take Daniel long to figure out that we would happily cater to his every whim – he only needed to give one of us a simple grunt or facial expression accompanied by some pointing and non-verbal cues. The three of us were totally over-sympathetic to his language barrier, and worked overtime to try and pinpoint each of his requests and needs. The first word Daniel ever spoke to Jimmy and me, within a few days of being in our presence was, "Dao!" I write it that way because I think it looks more Chinese, but he pronounced it like "Dow." Daniel used this expression often in China and at home too, and he used it in more ways than one. Mostly, he shouted it in a teasing manner when he was excited. In China, he and Jimmy would have "Dao" shouting wars across the bus aisle while Grandpa would hold Daniel in his lap. Daddy and Daniel both loved it.

We had no idea what he was saying, but it didn't matter to us as long as our son was happy – and laughing. For all Jimmy and I knew, he could have been calling us something horribly profane, and we would have still loved every minute of it. Daniel's other use of "Dao" was spoken in a more serious tone. The first time we experienced it was when we were in the Hong Kong airport waiting for our flight to Newark. I had gone to the food court, and there – like a beautiful mirage in the desert – I saw it: Popeye's Chicken and Biscuits.

Call me foolish for my love of an occasional junk food fix, but I think I actually drooled upon making my discovery (which, by the way, tasted heavenly after two weeks of eating authentic Chinese food). I came back to the seating area with a breakfast platter of scrambled eggs, bacon, a biscuit, and some darn yummy tater tots for all of us to share. As I reached my hand across the tray for a taste, Daniel shot me a look that could kill and bellowed, "DAO!" It was almost as if he wanted to say, "*Hands off Mommy – these are mine!*"

We never did figure out the true meaning of the word, even though we asked numerous people in China, and every one of them was as stumped as we were. During our fast food frenzy at the Hong Kong airport, there was a family seated with us, and the mother of the family was Chinese. I had mentioned Daniel's frequent use of the word and asked her if she knew the meaning, but she wasn't sure.

After she heard Daniel snap at me, however, it suddenly came to her. "He's saying *get away!*" she told me.

That had never occurred to me, but as I mulled it over, the meaning sort of made sense. Perhaps Daniel had been saying "get away" in a teasing and fun manner when joking with his Daddy, and had saved his most serious form of the word for when he was protecting his tater tots! From then on, I assumed that's what he meant, and Jimmy and I continued to joke with him. Daniel could go on for hours shouting "Dao!" back and forth with anyone and everyone who would willingly participate.

Other than that, Daniel's words were few and far between. We're still not sure – but suspect that it was probably due to the language barrier – which hadn't seemed to affect Madi, since she'd come to us as a one-year old baby and was not quite verbal yet. Occasionally, and much to our surprise, Daniel would blurt out an amazingly audible English word in his sweet little Elmo-like tone. I distinctly remember the way he said "hello." I loved how he rolled his little tongue to make the "L" sound, which is actually a pretty difficult sound to master for children, especially from China where they have completely different sounds and tones.

Jimmy had taught Daniel to say "my turn," which he would use outside in his swing. His version sounded more like "ma-tun," but he knew that it was the only way to get Jimmy to push him, so as Jimmy took turns pushing each of the kids, Daniel always gave it his very best effort. Like so many other parents, my husband and I relied on body language *a lot* – maybe too much, but we never wanted to put excessive pressure on our son. Jimmy and I wanted things to come to Daniel in *his own time*.

Chapter Nine

HALF THE SKY

$\mathcal{I}$ mentioned earlier that when we had arrived in China to bring Daniel home, we discovered (through Holt) that he had spent some time in the care of a wonderful organization called Half the Sky Foundation. We knew of them and had even donated to their cause in the past.

Half the Sky Foundation provides individual nurture and stimulation for babies, innovative preschools that encourage an early love of learning, personalized learning opportunities for older children, and permanent loving foster homes for children whose special needs will likely keep them from being adopted. From its small beginnings in the United States, Half the Sky Foundation has grown into an international community with charitable entities established in six major cities of the world, all dedicated to bringing the love and concern of family to thousands of orphaned children in China who have lost theirs.

Discovering that they had cared for our son was such a blessing, to say the least. Shortly after we arrived home, the Holy Spirit prompted me to contact Half the Sky Foundation to see if they had any available information about Daniel from when he had been in their care. Jimmy and I were elated when we received five progress reports via email! Can you imagine what it's like to have virtually no information or past history about your child, and then receive such a wealth of information? Jimmy and I knew that we would never be able to know every detail about our son, but finding out about that unknown time in his life meant the world to us. It was so miraculous to receive information that solved some of the mysteries of Daniel's past before he came into our family. The reports revealed that the nannies had obviously loved him and took very good care of him. And we were amazed to discover that Daniel had been taken into their care on September 19th, 2008 – Madi's birthday!

Here are the reports that we received from Half the Sky Foundation, which had been translated from their original Chinese versions:

FALL 2008

Hong Wei Feng, who has congenital heart disease, joined our program on September 19th, 2008. He was not afraid of the strangers and new environment. He just stared at me and then looked around the surroundings. I loved this beautiful boy at the first sight. He would smile whenever you amused him. Because he was rather weak, he was not able to sit steadily and he could raise his head for a little period of time when he lay on his back.

I have spent twenty days with him. During this period of time, he has received the treatment due to the bad health. When he turned a little better, we would sit and talk together. When I gave his body massage, he would look into my eyes. Then he would give me a sweet smile. How lovely he was. Now he is able to turn his body around the soft cushion. Moreover, he can sit alone for nearly one minute. When he sees a toy, he will reach out his hands to obtain it. After he gets it, he will have a close look at it. And he will shake it or knock at it. When his toy is taken by other children, he will cry sadly. He likes to play games with me and communicate with me face to face. Look at the photo! He was listening to me seriously.

WINTER 2008

Weifeng did not make much progress in this quarter. He got fever a few times and coughed. He knows to ask for food now. When he sees me holding a milk bottle, he will look at me and cry. Then as soon as I feed him, he will smile happily. Sometimes he will grab the bottle from me and hold it himself. He likes to lie on the foam mat, try to grab his little feet with his hands. When I amuse him, he will laugh out happily. He recognizes some of our voices. When he hears my voice, he will look at me and ask for a hug. If I do not take him, he will cry. He is able to think things over now. For example, when he sees a baby playing xylophone, he imitates her and striking the keyboard and then he hears the sound it makes. He thinks about it for a while and he understands that it this toy can make sound. When he sees me taking some snacks, he will extend his hands and ask for his share. He is so cute.

SPRING 2009

During this quarter, Weifeng was livelier. He can recognize people. When he sees people he likes, he will stretch out his hands and ask them to hug him. He no longer sits quietly. When he sits, he turns his body left and right to look around. When he sees things in front of him, he will try to move his body forwards to fetch them. When he lies on his stomach, he can push his torso off the ground for a while using his limbs. He can move his body left, right, and back. He can stand for a long time by holding one of my hands. He can switch the toys between his two hands to play. He can eat biscuits on his own. He can take the toys out of the containers. When

Weifeng sees the toys he likes not far away from him, he will crawl to them and then pick them up to play with. He is not very strong because of his ailment. He crawls for a while and then takes a break.

Weifeng likes playing games with me best. For example, I use the towel to cover his face and then uncover it to knock his head lightly with mine. We play games called 'clap your hands and touch your nose' (you can see it on the photo) and 'touch my head using yours.' He can imitate me by turning his wrist with music. When the music starts, the older children begin to swing left and right to dance. With an air of happiness, Weifeng looks at them excitedly and then begins to swing his body too. Then I stretch out my hands to him and he holds my hands to dance, with smile on his face. How happy is he! We teach him with games. Weifeng has been able to point out his nose and mouth. He can touch his head, clap his hands in welcome and wave goodbye.

Weifeng is more attached to me now. When he is happy, he will call me 'mom, mom' repeatedly. When he sees me hugging the other children, he will begin to cry loudly to show his unhappiness. Weifeng is a handsome and clever boy. We all like him.

SUMMER 2009

Weifeng has made great progress in this quarter. He is really active and cute. He can stand up by holding onto something and walk a few steps. He likes to stand by the table and pats on it. He is really good at crawling these days. He crawls around the activity room and looks for the toys or plays with other children. He is becoming more and more attached to me. When I play with him, he will not let me go or take care of other babies. He wants me to stay with him only or he will cry. He is smart and outgoing. He calls all the nannies mom and often smiles at them. He always observes our emotion. If someone looks at him with an upset expression, he will cry. Then if you give him a happy smile, he will laugh happily too. Weifeng likes new toys a lot. When we receive some new toys, he will always be the first to explore how to play with them.

FALL 2009

In this quarter, Weifeng has started to walk on his own without the help of walls or other things. He also likes to climb. When he plays with the rocking horse, he even stands on the back to swing. When he sees me scared or nervous about what he is doing, he will smile at me. What a mischievous boy! When he sees the other children climb upstairs, he will hold onto the railings to go upstairs and downstairs quickly. Weifeng has made progress in fine movement and he is more careful. He often pays attention to tiny objects. He is always interested in the screws on the mirror, windows, and shelves very much. He can play with them for a long time; he touches them and tries to turn them. Weifeng has better imitating ability now, and he can imitate the adults. For example, he can help me to hold the milk bottle for the younger girls to feed them.

He also calls me 'mom' on his own initiative. He calls me 'mom' before he does anything, and has established an inti-mate attachment to me. Every morning when he sees me, he will climb into my arms happily and be unwilling to leave me.

When he stays with me, he smiles all the time. Once I leave him, he will lie on the ground kicking and crying loudly. He is a smart boy; he can understand the expressions of the adults. He gets close to the people he likes; and smiles at everyone who plays with him. He is a very lovely and handsome boy!

The details in those reports verified so much about Daniel and his behaviors. They confirmed that he really was a good and very smart little boy. And they also confirmed, as I had suspected, that Daniel had developed a strong attachment to at least one of the nannies who'd cared for him.

As Daniel's true personality began to emerge, we could easily see that he was quite an independent little leader. It was evident that he didn't want to be thought of as a "baby." He insisted on doing everything – or *trying* to do everything – that Madi did, and I'm sure that's why he rejected his high chair instantly and demanded to sit in a chair at the table like the rest of us!

Daniel began to frequently imitate Madi, too. He had no idea what she was saying, but he would try so hard to mimic her exact words. At the dinner table, he would hold his hands in prayerful position and try to say grace with the rest of us. He would squeeze his eyes tightly shut, and pretend to know the words that the rest of us recited. There were a handful of times when Madi became frustrated with her "copycat" little brother, which always gave Jimmy and me a chuckle at Daniel's persistence.

Our son was a tremendous caregiver at heart. If he had a snack or a drink, he would make sure that everyone around him had one as well. Daniel would hand others their drink if he felt they needed or wanted it, because he always wanted to make sure that everyone around him was content. Our little angel was a very considerate child who was blessed with a generous heart.

Almost instantly, Daniel became an advocate for our three cats. As with most things that were unfamiliar to him, he approached them with caution. The cats were no exception, and Daniel took time to observe them from afar. But it wasn't long before he seemed to know their body language, and he would try to help them. One of our cats, Schroeder, was sick at the time and required special food. Daniel became aware of this through our actions, and he made it his job to protect Schroeder and his food bowl from our other two cats. Daniel took it upon himself to deliver their respective food bowls to each of them.

It began to bother Madi that there was a language barrier between her and Daniel, and even though he seemed to understand what she was (or we were) saying, Madi was frustrated that *she* couldn't understand *him*. When our social worker, Amy, came for our first post-placement visit, Madi discovered that we had a list of Chinese words and phrases in our possession to use for basic communication with Daniel. We had not been using the list, but realized that it might be a good idea for us to try.

Madi was adamant about reviewing the list that morning when I remembered that some of the Mei Mei's (Madi's adoptive Chinese friends I mentioned earlier) had started taking Chinese lessons while we were in China adopting Daniel. I called some of the mothers for more information about the classes, and we enrolled Madi the following week.

As I drove our daughter for her first lesson, I asked, "Madi, *why do you* want to learn Chinese?"

Madi intently replied, "So I will know what Daniel is saying, Mommy...so I will know what he needs." What a nurturing little soul she is.

Daniel had a devilish sense of humor and loved to be a little teaser. He spent many afternoons on our back patio with Daddy and his friend, Matt, as I carted Madi around to gymnastics and her various activities. The guys would tell us stories about Daniel's hilarious antics in our absence. For instance, Daniel would often confiscate Matt's cell phone and pretend to make calls. He would claim the phone as his own. I knew it was my fault for allowing Daniel to play with my cell phone from day one in China – just another fine example of how I over-indulged him! I have to give a shout out to Motorola for whatever phone model that was, because it must have been dropped more than a hundred times from a good distance. That thing bounced and shattered into pieces, but it still always seemed to work again. And every time it happened, I would curse myself for giving the phone to him…until the next time I gave in. It was a vicious cycle of Mommy buckling under to Daniel, who also loved playing with my car keys. It was not uncommon for our car alarm to go off whenever Daniel got hold of the keys and went right for that big, red panic button.

One day, Matt showed up at the house while Madi and I were gone, and Jimmy was in the shower. Daniel spotted him out on the patio and ran over to the glass door. He began pointing and trying to signal that Jimmy was in the shower. Daniel didn't know how to open the door, so he disappeared from the room and tore off into our bedroom. Matt knew that Daniel was desperately trying to make Jimmy aware of his visitor. Daniel would reappear at the glass, try to convey his message to Matt, run back and forth from the bedroom, point his determined little index finger in exasperation, and then grunt his way through an explanation. Matt got such a kick out of Daniel's enthusiastic efforts.

Our son had about one hundred nicknames. Okay, that's an exaggeration, but he did have a lot more than the average kid! Well, in the beginning, Daniel had become "Max" to Bubba and Grandpa, and it really stuck with them (as I previously mentioned). So much so that they asked us if it would be okay for them to continue calling him "Max" as their chosen nickname for him. Jimmy and I had no problem with it, and Daniel actually loved it when they called him Max! In fact, Madi called him Max in Bubba and Grandpa's presence, too!

Other than that, Madi almost always called her little brother "Daniel." Even from the get-go, when we intended to call him "DJ" as a nickname, Madi insisted that he was Daniel. Friends and family had bestowed a myriad of endearing nicknames upon our son, which included Dan Dan, Dan Yo Yo, Danny, Weifeng, Weifungus, the Funginator, DJ Feng, Butternut, Butternugget, Rosebud, and Benny Batzul. He was such a sweet and easygoing child that he embraced and responded to each of his nicknames. I think he just loved receiving so much positive attention from everyone around him that he couldn't have cared less.

Chapter Ten

SETTLING IN

On Monday, February 11th, Jimmy and I took Daniel for his first visit to the pediatric cardiologist's office in Boca Raton. The doctor was quite pleased to see Daniel's size. He was also pleased that the EKG and ultrasound results looked consistent with what was recorded on Daniel's medical reports. Nothing about our son's condition had been sugar-coated in his reports from China. Daniel was not happy being hooked up for the EKG, but he was totally calm for the ultrasound and barely moved a muscle so the cardiologist could successfully complete the task.

The pediatric cardiologist believed that Daniel's catheter procedure would likely be scheduled for March, and the results of the catheter procedure would confirm how and when the team would proceed surgically to correct Daniel's heart defects. When the cardiologist handed me the business card for our contact in Miami, I couldn't help but notice that the card was from a different hospital than our friends had been sent to with their young daughter. I didn't mention my concern at the time because I wasn't sure how the procedure worked. Maybe the catheter procedure would take place at a different hospital than the surgery?

When we got home and studied all the information, I emailed the cardiologist about our concerns. I really struggled with this because I had thought that we would be referred to a different cardiothoracic surgeon and hospital. The cardiologist replied to our email and explained that for the months since we'd brought Daniel's file to his office, this particular cardiothoracic team in Miami had been reviewing his file and formulating a plan to correct his condition. This hospital knew about Daniel and his case long before we'd even brought him home, and they were totally invested in his case. The cardiologist had also compared the two cardiothoracic surgeons in question, and paid them equal respect. He felt, however, that this particular surgeon – the one he had chosen to work with Daniel – would be preferable because of his post-surgery involvement and care with both his patients as well as their families. How could we argue with that? It certainly made sense to Jimmy and me.

I immediately began researching the recommended cardiothoracic surgeon, when I came across a section of his website called "Publications." As I scrolled through them – anxiously trying to rationalize our cardiologist's decision – I stumbled upon a study this surgeon had written with someone by the name 'Feng.'

I thought it was odd to make such an interesting discovery, since Feng was part of Daniel's Chinese name. I continued to scroll down and came across something even more intriguing – numerous publications written *with* someone named D.J. Murphy! Seriously? I was stunned by the mere coincidence.

All of a sudden, a tranquil feeling coursed through my veins (and my heart) that Daniel was scheduled at the right place, with the right team, and that this was *no coincidence*. At that moment, and as I continued my research, I no longer felt the desperate need to pursue other medical options.

That same week in February, my Dad's brother, Uncle Johnny (a.k.a. "Opa") and Aunt Donnie came to visit from New Jersey. They had such a great time with the kids and instantly connected with Daniel. Opa is one of those fun-loving people who adores children. Perhaps it's because he's pretty much a big kid himself. Opa is famous for getting the kids all fired up – especially right before bedtime when they just become sleepy and begin to rub their tired little eyes. Aunt Donnie is constantly on his case for this impish behavior, but Opa can't seem to help himself. Around here we live by the saying, "Don't poke the bear" if you know what I mean! Leave those sleepy kids alone – at least long enough for me (a.k.a. "Mom") to enjoy some adult conversation over a glass of wine! It was all in good fun though, and the kids adored playing with him.

We celebrated Valentine's Day with them and Grandpa Murphy at Bubba and Grandpa's house and simply enjoyed our family time. Grandpa was so happy to present the kids with their Valentine's gifts – a stuffed Dora doll for Madi and a stuffed character named Pablo from the Backyardigans show for Daniel. Madi already owned more than a few Dora dolls, most of which had come from Bubba and Grandpa previously – but sweet Madi graciously accepted the doll and thanked Grandpa with a wide grin. Daniel snatched his Pablo doll from Grandpa and hugged it tightly – for all of two seconds. Then he promptly cast the doll to the ground and marched away!

Our son's reaction was so comical to Jimmy and me because we knew that Daniel simply wasn't used to having his own toys, so they really didn't seem to carry that much importance to him. Daniel just didn't seem to value possessions so much in his new environment.

That Valentine's Day was the first time that Bubba and Daniel truly bonded. Bubba had given Daniel a lot of space the first week because she really wanted him to warm up to her on his own terms.

I know it must have been difficult for her, but the timing was so perfect. That night, it was magical to watch them as he sat on her lap and she fed him yogurt for a good twenty minutes. She wiped his face after every messy bite (which made him tremendously content), and he was so relaxed that he nearly fell asleep eating.

Bubba and Daniel

Four days later, Jimmy and I made our first visit to the emergency room with one of our kids. Daniel had rolled off Bubba and Grandpa's bed while we were at their house for dinner to celebrate Bubba's birthday. Yes, with three adults present in the room (my husband makes it clear to point out that *he* was not there), Daniel was engaged in playing, and somehow managed to barrel-roll right off the bed in the excitement! As parents everywhere know, it's amazing (and frightening) how quickly these accidents can happen right under your nose.

After the fall, Daniel seemed to favor his right arm and was really having a difficult time getting comfortable. Jimmy managed to comfort him and get him to sleep that night, but my husband's fatherly intuition (as well as a long history of sports injuries) told him that there was probably more to this story.

At about 9:00 p.m., Daniel woke up crying and his arm appeared much more swollen. I called our trusty pediatrician, Dr. Bradford (who, thankfully, *always* answers his phone), and he suggested that we take Daniel to the nearest emergency room. Bubba, who is always there to help out in a pinch, immediately came to our house to watch Madi while Jimmy and I headed to the hospital with Daniel.

Our son was such a little trooper despite the circumstances. The three of us sat in the emergency room at Bethesda Memorial Hospital in Boynton Beach for a couple of hours. There we were, late at night, as medical professionals took x-rays and asked us a million questions about how the incident happened.

It was an exhausting interview. Jimmy and I secretly suspected they were trying to figure out if we had hurt Daniel so they could report us to the Department of Children and Families. Thankfully, we passed their inquisition in short time, and after studying several x-rays they had taken, the doctor confirmed that our son had fractured his right elbow. We were discharged with a sling on Daniel's arm, and it was well after midnight when we arrived home. But even as exhausted as he was, Daniel remained his same happy-go-lucky self; he was just thrilled to be home.

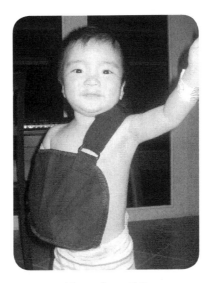

Home from E.R.

Over the course of the next day, Daniel's hand began to appear bluish in color. Since it just didn't look right to me, I decided to take him to our pediatrician for an emergency visit – only to discover that his arm had been wrapped too tightly at the hospital the night before. The pediatrician on staff recommended that we take Daniel to an orthopedic doctor as soon as possible, but – unfortunately – there was a scramble to get Daniel's medical records from the hospital over to our pediatrician's office on Friday. And by the time they received the records, it was simply too late to be referred to an orthopedic doctor.

The pediatrician did not want us to wait over the weekend without seeing someone, so he instructed us to drive down to the emergency room at Joe DiMaggio Children's Hospital in Hollywood. Jimmy and I first drove back to the original hospital in Boynton Beach to pick up Daniel's x-rays, and then the three of us headed south to Hollywood (which was about 45 minutes away). Thankfully, Bubba saved the day again and came to our house to watch Madi.

After all the turmoil, the hospital, unfortunately, did not have an orthopedic doctor on staff that night, but they were able to take additional x-rays and apply a better splint on Daniel's arm, so at least it wasn't a totally wasted trip. We were finally home by 10:00 p.m., and Daniel – once again – proved to be a real trooper.

Back in the E.R.

On Saturday, February 20th (the next morning), we celebrated Daniel's rite of baptism at St. Vincent Ferrer Catholic Church. The week before at Mass, we'd run into our "Family Deacon," Deacon Lee and his lovely wife, Alice. They are wonderful people who had guided Jimmy and me through our Rite of Christian Initiation for Adults (RCIA) process at St. Vincent Ferrer Catholic Church in 2006.

Since Deacon Lee had baptized Madi, we had our hearts set on him baptizing Daniel, too. The morning that we'd bumped into him at Mass, Deacon Lee quickly pulled out his calendar and was adamant that we christen Daniel right away – like less than a week away! Deacon Lee made sure the church was cleared for us on the following Saturday. Since we'd spent the previous night in the emergency room, Jimmy and I expected Daniel to be very tired and probably a bit cranky, but given our son's medical issues and his latest accident, we felt it was the best idea to proceed as planned, so we expedited Daniel's baptism, broken arm and all.

We chose Aunt Sheila (Jimmy's cousin) and her husband, David, as Daniel's Godparents. When their oldest son, Murphy, found out, he excitedly asked his Mom, "Does that make me Daniel's God brother?" It was comforting to know that Daniel was blessed with an entire supportive God family to guide him.

Among a small gathering of family and close friends, our son's baptism was such a touching service. A special reserve of Holy Water from the Jordan River in Israel (the same body of water in which Jesus was baptized by John) was shared by Deacon Lee. It brought tears to my eyes that Daniel should be blessed in such an extra special way. I remember feeling – and stating – that it was truly the most beautiful baptism I had ever witnessed. In spite of a couple of long nights at the hospital (and an obvious fear of water), Daniel handled the baptism beautifully, almost as if he knew what it were all about, and perhaps felt the hand of God upon him. It was a joyous day.

Baptism

Chapter Eleven

DAILY LIFE

As our family gradually settled back into our daily life, I wanted Daniel's routine to be more entertaining than just driving Madi to and from school and/or her activities. I must say, though, that the school "car line" was a very special time for both of them. Each morning, Madi would sweetly kiss her brother goodbye as she exited the van, and when Daniel and I would pick her up from her speech classes at Banyan Creek Elementary, they were equally excited to see each other after being apart.

At Madi's preschool, Daniel enjoyed walking her into the classroom so much that it became a challenge to get him to leave! Daniel would always pucker up for Madi's teacher, Mrs. Bivins, and sometimes she would graciously give him something to take with him as a "consolation" for having to leave!

Jimmy and I really looked forward to the day when Daniel would be in her classroom as a student because it seemed as if he were already up for the challenge. When Daniel and I would pick Madi up, he would run into the classroom to collect her, and they would embrace in a bear hug as if they hadn't seen each other for years. During the months before we traveled to China, I had only imagined those affectionate moments and how incredibly rewarding it was to now witness the loving exchanges between them. The two played beautifully together, so much so that neighbors began to remark how they loved hearing the jubilant sounds that emanated from our backyard.

When our schedules permitted, my "stay-at-home-mom" status allowed me to take Daniel to a Mommy & Me class at the YMCA. On more than a few occasions (after a restless night), Daniel would fall asleep on the way to the class, and I would turn the van around and head back home. Daniel and I did manage to make it to a few sessions, but I never wanted to push him too much.

When we did make it, his favorite part of the class was definitely "bubble time." Daniel would pursue a bubble until he caught it on his finger, and then he would just stare at it in sheer awe and study it. Shortly thereafter, he would try to eat it. Daniel was so completely fascinated by bubbles that I think he could have been happy with only having "bubble time." At the end of the class, he would sit so quietly in my lap and wait patiently for his hand stamp. Daniel was so cute with the other children, too. When I would prompt him to say "goodbye" to his friends after class, Daniel would walk over to each child, one by one, and give each of them a little wave. It was obvious that he had been well socialized in China.

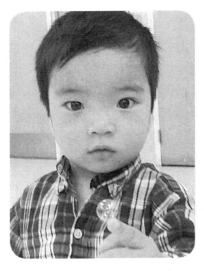

Bubble time at Mommy & Me

Daniel and I stayed home in the mornings on most days and just bonded together. He loved to help me load and unload the dishwasher, and he also enjoyed helping me with the laundry. It seemed that Daniel just wanted to feel like part of the housekeeping process, so I kindly indulged him! I cherish those times with our son – he was such a good little helper.

On occasion, Daniel would also come along to Madi's gymnastics classes. The studio owner, Miss Jody – who is such a wonderful, loving person – even formed a Mommy and Me class for the little ones who were forced to wait for their older siblings in the lobby. Miss Jody was so kind and patient with Daniel. The first time he went to the studio, she "broke the ice" by rolling a little soccer ball to him, and they bonded instantly. In no time, Daniel was fully engaged and laughing. Miss Jody was such a natural at teasing with him, too, which he clearly loved. Daniel enjoyed his classes there, and I can still picture him running towards me at his full speed during the relay races. He was so happy and obviously loved the chance to run freely. When Daniel would get close to the finish line, he would turn around and run the other way as if the game had switched directions, and with the biggest grin on his face.

Sadly, we didn't make it to many of those classes because it seemed that we were always preparing for a medical procedure, and I felt the need to shield Daniel from as many germs as possible during those times. The blessing was that, while Madi and I went on our way, Daniel spent all of those afternoons bonding and playing with Bubba and Grandpa. They adored Daniel, and he adored them, too.

One day in particular, Madi and I returned to find Daniel sound asleep on the floor of their back patio where he was covered with a fuzzy, tiger-striped blanket. Apparently, he had been fighting his nap, so Bubba and Grandpa just let Daniel tire himself out. Eventually, he plopped down next to the blanket, fell asleep right there, and slept soundly (on the floor) for about two hours!

Jimmy and I are so thankful for the time Daniel spent growing close to them at their home. Grandpa – who was known to be somewhat grumpy with young children, and never seemed to quite understand them – had developed such a soft spot for him. There was something about Daniel that truly intrigued him – he saw Daniel as a survivor.

Perhaps it was also Daniel's zeal and enthusiasm for just about everything in sight, and the knowledge that his survival was against all odds. Daniel somehow made you think about things in a different way, and Grandpa found it difficult to be angry with him. Even when his grandson would slam their bedroom door in fun, Grandpa was furious until he discovered that it was Daniel's doing. Then – somehow – it wasn't so offensive to him!

Grandpa with Madi and Daniel

Daniel loved to push Madi's baby doll stroller all around their house with her baby doll in it. The doll made cooing sounds like a real baby, and that totally fascinated Daniel because he was such a nurturing little guy. He would stare at the baby doll in total disbelief as he tried to figure out how that doll was talking! Bubba would spend hours in the playroom having tea parties with the kids, which they both loved. Bubba would let Madi and Daniel mix sugar and water in their toy teapot, and allowed them to go crazy as they spilled water everywhere. The kids would get covered in their concoction, and everything in the room would get wet, too. I love that Bubba just didn't care. Thankfully, Grandpa usually had no idea what was happening back in that playroom, or he would have been in complete meltdown mode over the mess!

For the most part, though, Daniel was a neat freak – just like his Grandpa. He was so funny, and it seemed apparent that he had been catered to in China. During meals, if he had a spot of yogurt or food on his mouth, he would pucker his little lips and grunt as if to say, "Someone please clean this up!"

Daniel was such a terribly picky eater, which was quite troubling to us as parents. Madi had always enjoyed eating, so this was totally foreign territory. We wondered if his eating (or lack thereof) was a control issue. He'd had so little control of everything else going on in his life that perhaps his refusal to eat was his way to exercise his limited ability to take control. We knew this was a probability, and who could blame him? So when it came to food, we ended up totally indulging Daniel. It seemed crazy that I was making extra meals for him just to see whether or not he would eat them. Jimmy and I found it so frustrating, but we totally accommodated him because we knew good nutrition was imperative to keeping him healthy.

Daniel would routinely eat foods with the same baby-food consistency (like oatmeal, cream of wheat, and grits), and he was still crazy about yogurt. We often joked that if the "Make a Wish Foundation" ever called, Daniel's wish would be for the Stonyfield Farm Truck to pull up and drop off a lifetime supply of their Yo-Baby yogurt drinks! Jimmy and I actually had to stop buying them (often) because when Daniel knew that they were in our refrigerator, he wouldn't stop yanking on the door until he drank every last one! Yo-Baby yogurt drinks quickly became Daniel's special treat at Bubba and Grandpa's house because we simply couldn't afford to support his habit!

Bubba would also feed our son popsicles to his heart's content. All Daniel had to do was point his little index finger at the freezer and (because Bubba couldn't resist) she would give him three or four popsicles in a day – no wonder he loved being over there!

Thankfully, I could also count on Daniel to eat his Juice Plus+® gummies consistently (to offset the popsicles), which came as a relief. He would take me by the hand, lead me to the counter where we stored them, and he would dance and throw his fists in the air for gummies. I was giving Daniel twice the recommended daily dosage, but it was totally worth the cost, because I would do anything to get fruits and veggies into that baby's body! He loved them so much that Madi would frequently use them as a way to get Daniel out of her bedroom. The second he entered her "off-limits" room, Madi would holler, "Gummy time!" and Daniel would make a beeline to the kitchen shrieking with joy. I had found myself obsessed with Daniel's eating habits – one of *my own* "control issues."

PROGRESS IN THE FOOD DEPARTMENT | Mar. 11, 2010

Daniel has graduated from his high chair. As much as I'd like to keep him captive, he indicated - through pointing and various verbal clues - that he wanted to sit in a big chair like the rest of us. So far, so good with one exception - he fell off the chair and landed on his side the other night. Poor little guy is so reckless. We have continued to indulge his "big boy" desires, but we're watching him a bit more closely. I think a booster seat may be in his near future!

Daniel has refused most of the foods that we've offered to him. He won't even try a bite of some things, and it's frustrating because we know he would love some of them! Yesterday seems to have been a turning point. He tried four new things without disappointment, so maybe he'll trust our offers a bit more.

This morning the trend continued. I put a whole grain waffle in front of him (and Madi), and he ate the whole thing! Nothing satisfies a mother like seeing your child eat well (at least this mother).

It gives Jimmy and me immense joy that Daniel was able to experience so much in such a short time. He attended his first official American-style party to celebrate the birthday of our Mei Mei friend, Ami Mei. The party took place at Miss Jody's gymnastics studio (that Daniel was quite familiar with), which made him very comfortable. Madi loved showing off her little brother to everyone in our special Mei Mei group. Daniel thoroughly enjoyed interacting with all the kids and sat at the "big kid's table" to eat snacks and indulge in Ami's birthday cake. He joyfully received his first goodie bag on our way out!

In the company of his God brothers, Murphy and Myles, Daniel got to bang on Murphy's drums (he actually seemed to have quite good rhythm) and even played on a bongo set that once belonged in the band *Santana*. Now how many toddlers get a chance to do that?!

Playing drums with Murphy

It has been an annual tradition of ours to go to St. Vincent Ferrer's Spring Festival, and it was pretty special having our son there with us. Daniel rode a carousel for the first time, and even went on the Ferris wheel with Jimmy, which was a "first" for Madi, too. I must admit that I was *terrified* for Daniel, especially when I saw his little face peek over the edge of the ride at the highest point in the sky!

I love that Jimmy encouraged Daniel to be a "boy." Jimmy never let Daniel's health condition affect his daily activities, and I truly admire that about him. I, on the other hand, sometimes treated Daniel like a piece of delicate porcelain. I was so nervous that he would get hurt that I was almost in a constant state of anxiousness. I suppose it didn't help that Daniel was such a clumsy little guy, who always seemed to manage to – even before we left China – take a few tumbles. Well, Jimmy would hang Daniel upside down by his ankles. And our son loved it when Daddy would rough-house and throw him around like a sack of potatoes (even though it made me a nervous wreck!) Jimmy and Madi taught Daniel how to stand on the swings and climb up the slide in our backyard. He even climbed the rock wall a few times.

It made Daniel so happy to do all the things that a completely healthy child would, and it gives me so much pleasure to know that (thanks to his father) our son was able to experience the joy of being an active little boy. You could see that Daniel would tire easily, but he tenaciously refused to stop or give up.

Carousel ride with Daddy

♡

Chapter Twelve

MEDICAL PROCEDURES

The month of March brought more follow-up trips to the orthopedic doctor to x-ray Daniel's arm and monitor his healing process. His fracture seemed to be healing well, much to our satisfaction, but Daniel's cast had to come off before any other major medical procedures could take place.

To pass time in the doctor's office exam room, I would entertain Daniel by tearing off small pieces of paper from the exam table cover, roll them into little balls, and ask him to throw them away for me. I could then relax for a few minutes and watch him try to figure out how to operate the trash can lid with the foot pedal. It certainly kept him busy while we waited. By our last visit, he had finally figured out how to step on the lever and open the lid by himself.

Daniel's cast came off on March 19th, about one month after it had been put on. His reaction to its removal was interesting – almost as if he had cast separation anxiety when they took it away. I had never been involved in the removal of a cast before, so I couldn't even begin to imagine my son's thoughts as he watched the buzz saw that was coming toward his arm. It seemed like such a primitive method to remove a cast! I kept Daniel calm, and he was actually very, very good while the nurse removed it. In truth, he handled it much better than I did, but I took a deep breath and remained calm for my son's sake. The orthopedic doctor gave us strict instructions to keep Daniel "in a bubble" for the next two weeks while his arm was still tender. That task seemed impossible for obvious reasons! This adorable picture was taken at the doctor's office after his cast was removed. Daniel was wearing his sister's headband, which he adored. Madi had refused to let him wear it before, so on this day, he was in his glory!

Modeling Madi's headband

Daniel had developed such a bright spirit that it was almost as if he were magnetic. People seemed to be drawn to him wherever we would go. Of course, he *was* pretty darn cute – but there was something more, something intriguingly wise about him. For example, the day that we were in the doctor's office waiting to have his cast removed, Daniel bonded with a kind, elderly gentleman in the waiting room. The two exchanged smiles and handshakes and seemed to connect right away. The man asked me many questions about Daniel and his adoption, to which I answered openly.

When he was leaving the office with his family, the gentleman pulled out a five-dollar bill from his wallet and handed it to Daniel with strict instructions to buy himself something fun. Well, Daniel certainly didn't know much about the value of money, but he was obviously aware that it was something special because he grabbed that bill as if it were the winning lottery ticket! I thanked that generous man profusely and couldn't believe what kindness I had witnessed from a complete stranger. I will never forget it.

Daniel's catheter procedure was originally scheduled for Friday, March 26th. The hospital had warned us that if he had any symptoms of a cold or sickness, they would not be able to proceed. Daniel had a little bit of a cough that week, which didn't seem serious, but it had crossed my mind to contact the cardiologist about it. The office decided that they would rather wait until Monday to make sure that Daniel wasn't coming down with something. Jimmy and I were disappointed at first, and I was even mad at myself for possibly overreacting and calling them, but we have always believed that things happen for a reason. The delay just meant that our trip to Miami on Sunday would be a bit more relaxed, and since Madi would be on Spring Break that week, she would still be able to go with us.

When she woke up Sunday morning, Madi hollered, "Gratulations, Daniel! You're going for your heart surgery!" Despite a few sibling ups and downs, the kids were great travel companions. On the drive to Miami, Daniel dropped his toy too far out of reach for any of us to retrieve. After a few moments, Madi handed him *her* toy and said, "Today is all about you, Daniel, *my* little brudder."

We arrived at our hotel in Miami at around 4:00 p.m. on Sunday. It was enough time to settle into our room and head down to the hotel restaurant for a quick bite to eat. It was a little tricky getting the kids to sleep that night because they were excited and obviously a little out of sorts with their surroundings. Jimmy and I had faith that Daniel would be fine, but inside we were a little scared – not so much because of the procedure, but more out of concern for Daniel's inability to comprehend what was happening to him or why. We just didn't want our son to be frightened.

The next morning, we left the hotel at 6:30 a.m. and headed over to the children's hospital. We arrived at the P.I.R.R. (Patient Intake and Recovery Room) on the 5th Floor at 7:00 a.m. sharp. Since Daniel had not been allowed any food or drink after midnight, Jimmy and I decided that all of us should refrain from food or drink until our son was admitted to the catheter lab. Knowing that Daniel was quite hungry and thirsty, and that he was slated as the second procedure of the day (not the first), the nurses offered him some apple juice. In our heads, Jimmy and I both questioned this decision, but we trusted the nurses and kept our mouths shut. Shortly thereafter, we heard rumblings that patient #1 hadn't shown up, and Daniel could now go first. But unfortunately, our son had already consumed the apple juice that the nurses gave him and now had to wait four hours for the juice to clear his system. My husband and I weren't very pleased about that, and neither was the Director of Catheterization.

Finally at about 12:30 p.m., they proceeded with administering Daniel's IV, and Jimmy was right beside him. Thankfully, Madi and I weren't present to witness that mess. Evidently, they had a problem finding his little veins and – after poking his hands numerous times – finally resorted to using a special ultrasound that could help to locate his veins. When Jimmy brought Daniel back, his sweet little face was wet with tears, and Jimmy was on the verge of crying, as well.

About half an hour later, the anesthesiologists (who were both instantly terrific with our baby) came to sedate Daniel and take him into the catheter lab. That was the first time we met Amanda, whom you'll read more about later in this story. At one point, Daniel had three stethoscopes in his possession because he showed such fascination with them that the doctors would just hand them over to make him feel more comfortable. The anesthesiologists even filled a syringe with saline solution and allowed Daniel to put it into his IV so he would think he was administering his own medicine! A few short minutes later, it was apparent that his little world was spinning.

After several hours and many trips to the vending machines (Madi's favorite part of a hospital visit), we were brought the good news from the Director of Catheterization herself. Not only was Daniel fine, but they were very optimistic about his pulmonary system! They were pleased to find two very strong arteries, and only two collateral vessels had formed – that they found, anyway. One of these vessels, on the left, was what they originally thought was "patent ductus arteriosus (PDA)." The ductus arteriosus is a blood vessel that is an essential part of fetal blood circulation. Within minutes – or even up to a few days – after birth, the vessel is supposed to close as part of the normal changes that occur in a baby's circulatory system.

Though his PDA had been diagnosed as "open" in China, Daniel's had actually closed, and the collateral vessel that had formed in his body was transporting all the oxygen to Daniel's lungs and sustaining his life! There was another small vessel on the right side, but it had narrowed significantly and wasn't functioning effectively, so the surgical team closed it off. They also learned that a portion of the lower lobe of Daniel's right lung had been permanently damaged from lack of oxygenation, but they were very optimistic about what they had seen inside Daniel's chest, and the team planned to discuss his case at the next catheter conference to decide when they would proceed surgically.

It took a while to calm Daniel down after the procedure as his anesthesia began to wear off. But because we (thankfully) had been warned by several people about the adverse reactions of kids coming off anesthesia, we were prepared – though I don't know if one can ever be fully prepared for that experience. Daniel was strong as an ox, and he was not a happy boy; he was quite ornery, actually, and it took all of Jimmy's strength to keep Daniel somewhat horizontal. By the time they released him from the recovery room (two hours later), it was after 6:00 p.m. The staff required Daniel to stay for the night so they could observe him. Our brave little boy finally settled into a hospital room shortly after 7:00 p.m., and Jimmy and I decided that I should stay overnight with Daniel while he and Madi drove home in hopes of a good night's rest.

Daniel and I had a long night of little sleep in the hospital. It seemed like he would just nod off, and then someone on staff would come in the room to take his vitals or poke him. It was so irritating, though I knew that the hospital was the best possible place for us to ensure that our son was recovering properly. At one point, I yelled at the nurse in frustration for waking Daniel up yet again, and I later had to apologize for losing my cool with her. Thankfully, the nurse understood that all I wanted was for Daniel to get some rest.

The next morning, Daniel and I woke at about 5:00 a.m., and after he was examined and given a good report, I was relieved that he was discharged at 10:00 a.m. Jimmy (with Madi) drove down to pick us up, and Daniel and I both passed out on the way home! Our little boy was fabulous – fabulous and resilient – and Madi was pretty brave herself. What she witnessed – watching as her little brother came out of anesthesia – was pretty brutal, but she handled it amazingly well. It appeared as though she had developed a new-found appreciation (and level of protection) for her little brother, as well as a new respect for his bravery level. From that day forward, anytime Madi was hurt, she would call out for Daniel to console her! It cracked us up that she would call on her two-year old little brother for comfort, but Madi had seen Daniel go through so much physically, and she was well-aware that he knew what pain was all about.

On April 12th, Daniel's surgical team met to discuss his case at the catheter conference, and they scheduled his surgery for May 11th. That date seemed so far off in the distance to us. Jimmy and I felt so conflicted, because part of us wanted his surgery to be done right away, but the other part of us believed that the timing was better for bonding purposes. I can remember nights in Daniel's bed when I would hear wheezing and crackling sounds in his breathing, and his heart felt like it was literally going to jump out of his skin. On those occasions, I felt so fearful and paranoid that he wouldn't survive until the surgery. Overall though, Jimmy and I were satisfied that the surgery date would give Daniel another month to adjust to his new life, and we believed that it was soon enough to get his heart condition expeditiously corrected. In hindsight, we are so thankful for every extra second of time we had with him.

Before catheterization

Chapter Thirteen

CHALLENGES

Even though he had a water-bearer Zodiac sign (Aquarius), Daniel had a sort of "love-hate" relationship with water. Our son disliked taking a bath or shower at all, so Jimmy and I struggled with bathing from the get-go in China. Once we got home, we both tried to get him into the tub without success for several months.

As Daniel stood outside the tub and watched Madi, Jimmy and I would clean him with a washcloth while he splashed her bath water with his hands. We would shampoo his hair and then hold him over the tub to rinse his head. Daniel didn't particularly love that either, but for him it was better than the alternative choice of actually taking a bath. Daniel loved playing with Madi, but not enough to get in that tub with her! He got lucky with both his arm cast and his catheterization wounds because – per doctor's orders – he wasn't allowed to get them wet.

Jimmy and I were concerned and perplexed by Daniel's behavior: Was he actually afraid of the water? Had something happened to our son to traumatize him so? Or was this merely a control issue? Daniel appeared to be absolutely terrified when we would dip his feet in the tub. I did, however, notice that he had other "sensitivity issues" with his feet, too. In both the sand box and the grass, Daniel never liked to be barefoot, and he would always insist that I put his sneakers on him.

We were finally able to get Daniel into the bathtub for the first time on April 15th, and it was actually Bubba who managed to get the job done. Jimmy and I certainly weren't proud of the fact that it had taken us so long, but we were reluctant to push the issue with him. My husband and I cut Daniel a lot of slack in many ways. On one night, while I left the kids at Bubba and Grandpa's house for a few minutes and delivered some dinner home to Jimmy, I could hardly believe my eyes when I returned.

To my amazement, Bubba's arms were tightly grasped around Daniel's belly, and he was perched on the edge of the tub with his feet dangling in the water. Bubba slowly began to lower Daniel into the tub so he could finally feel his feet on the bottom. That was the first time our son had expressed any sincere desire to get into the water. For two months, he'd spent his time on the "sidelines" watching Madi in the tub and playing with his toys from the outside. That made Jimmy and me wonder if maybe – all that time – he thought the tub was really deep. Once Daniel felt the bottom, he slid himself down so he could sit in the tub.

Madi loved that her brother was finally in there with her, and she proudly hollered, "Gratulations, Daniel! Gratulations, Big Boy!" Once he conquered his fear, Daniel enjoyed his daily bath, and it soon became a challenge to get him out! He loved the bubbles and busily played with his stacking cups. Daniel also loved washing himself, especially his belly (which – after three months of good food – was protruding quite a bit). It was obvious that he was very proud of overcoming his fear.

In the bathtub!

Daniel was equally skeptical about swimming pools. Jimmy and I really didn't worry too much about him falling in a pool because he kept such a safe distance. I am thankful for the fond memories of two occasions when I was able to get him in the pool and was then able to move around with him in my arms. Daniel was not exactly "comfortable," but I loved swirling him around in the water and consoling him. I loved how he would cling to me so tightly, as if he were holding on for dear life.

And while we're on the subject of water, Daniel also took issue with rain. There were several occasions – perhaps coming home from an errand or playing out on our back patio – when it began to rain. Daniel was literally paralyzed with fear by the rain. He would just stand there, as stunned as a deer in the headlights, and then he would start to cry until one of us scooped him up and carried him inside the house.

Interestingly though, one of Daniel's favorite things was to run water out of the sink faucet. He loved to wash his hands and brush his teeth excessively, which would drive Madi absolutely crazy since she has been raised with me on her case not to waste water. She would holler to me from the bathroom because Daniel wouldn't listen to her when she told him to turn off the faucet. Once again, Daniel got a free pass from Mommy. I usually indulged him for a little bit before I'd shut the water off.

Sleeping was another tough battle for Daniel. I am not proud to admit that I lost my temper with him on several occasions – almost always over sleeping issues – since Jimmy and I, too, had become seriously sleep deprived during that time. Like so many other parents, we grew really frustrated by Daniel's unwillingness to simply lie down and sleep. We could totally relate to the bestselling children's book parody for tired parents called "Go the _____ to Sleep," by Adam Mansbach.

Each weekday, Daniel and I would pick Madi up from school, and after lunch I would lay the kids down to watch a movie in our bed so they could have their quiet time. Daniel wanted to do everything that Madi did, and I knew that if he would only stay still long enough, he would fall asleep. But that was the problem – Daniel loved to torment his sister during movie time. He would roll around on our bed, throw his legs all over Madi, and totally invade her space until she was (justifiably) irritated. I was so thankful that Madi understood this was my only chance to get a nap time for Daniel, so she would graciously put up with it all, God bless her.

After giving Daniel two warnings that he would have to go to his room, there was – almost always – a third offense (this became our daily routine). I would carry him to his room and put him down on his bed, at which point he would break down in tears and physically try to get back to Madi. Somehow, (after scolding him) I would cave every single day and take him back into our bedroom because I hated to hear my son cry. After going back and forth on our "nap dance," Daniel would finally give up and fall asleep in our bed. At that point, Madi knew that she was free to go play in her room.

I knew it was my fault for condoning Daniel's behavior and for failing to discipline him, but there was something inside me that was absolutely powerless when it came to disciplining him. Given Daniel's medical condition, I was reluctant to upset him. I believed there would be plenty of time for disciplining him after his surgery took place and his heart condition was corrected. In my heart, I suppose I felt pity for Daniel, and sadly, at times, I failed to do the right thing as a mother, which was to simply give him the discipline that he needed.

My frustration over Daniel's inability to sleep usually resulted in me losing my patience, and shouting at him, which would make him even more upset. I remember one time in particular when I screamed so loudly that Daniel's crying escalated, and then I started crying, too. I just wanted him to stop. I just wanted my son to listen to me, but he wouldn't, so I lost my temper and failed to respond to him in the loving way that he needed me to. I fell short of the grace so freely given by our Lord. I remember all of a sudden having this intense feeling – almost like a premonition, but more like a fleeting primal fear – that I should appreciate that moment, and I sensed that I should treasure holding Daniel right then and there because God could take that moment away at any time, and God could take Daniel away at any time, too.

I cried and hugged him so tightly and apologized to him over and over for failing him, and then I apologized to God for losing control and for taking it out on Daniel. It's interesting that I hated to hear my baby cry, yet my actions and my lack of control made me do something that made him cry even more. We all have our demons, and control is one of mine. God knows *I wish I had* embraced every moment, but at times I allowed my impatience and anger to get the best of me. I am only human, and I'm well aware of my weaknesses but losing my patience with Daniel is something I will always regret. I am comforted only by the fact that Daniel knew I loved him immensely – this I know in my heart.

Daniel's nights were equally stressful, and he frequently woke up. Either Jimmy or I usually managed to get him to sleep at around 7:00 p.m., following the same bedtime routine as Madi had. Sometimes it was a struggle, but one of us would stay with him until he'd fall asleep. Since Daniel naturally slept with his eyelids half open, it was also a challenge to make sure that he was really asleep. We would have to wave our hands in front of his face to be sure, and this was a risky move until we felt fairly certain that our son was no longer awake. Jimmy and I would try to get to bed early each night in anticipation of Daniel's first wake-up call, which would take place around 10:00 p.m.

I could hear his initial stirs, and I became a pro at knowing the slightest sounds of movement on the monitor. By the time Daniel would begin crying, I could usually make it down the hallway to greet him at his bedroom door. Sometimes I could scoop him up and get him back into bed, but that usually didn't happen. He would grunt and point his finger down the hallway toward the kitchen. I would end up carrying him into the kitchen, plopping him down on the kitchen counter and then try to figure out how to appease him. I think this was a control thing, too, and God knows Daniel had my number! I would routinely pull out a yogurt and some juice for him – he didn't require much. He just wanted to make sure that

I would provide for him. After a few minutes, I was able to pick Daniel up and carry him back to his bedroom without protest.

Back in his room, I would hold him for a while to comfort him, and he would cry if I tried to put him down before he was ready. On occasion, Daniel would fall asleep quickly, and I could lay him back down within five to ten minutes to get the rest that his body so desperately needed. But if I tried to lay him down too soon for his liking, it was pandemonium. The second he would feel his feet touch the bed, Daniel would start wailing. Sometimes I would have to hold him for what seemed like an eternity, just because he was so darn heavy. Once again, my patience was tested, and I failed to do the right thing at times. There was one night in particular when I blurted out so many profanities that Jimmy yelled at me and told me Daniel was going to think his name was (insert bleeps here). Side note: when my husband was a boy, he often thought his name was "Dammit Jimmy."

In retrospect, we often wonder if perhaps it was physically uncomfortable for Daniel to lie down. Perhaps the horizontal position put extra stress on his lungs and made it difficult for him to breathe? Or maybe lying down was painful for him after awhile. Was it possible that he could actually feel a lack of oxygen through his body when he was horizontal? We asked ourselves these questions over and over again.

Sometimes Daniel would take my hand and put it to his chest, as if he were showing me that it hurt and that he needed me to rub his chest. It is also plausible that his body was extremely fatigued from being so active throughout the day. Our son was probably much more active – given his condition – than his body should have been. Jimmy and I can speculate now, but we will never know.

Of course, my husband and I also wondered if waking up alone is what scared Daniel. At the time, that is what we instinctively thought since we knew that he'd slept in a bed with Clara in China. There were many nights – in fact, most nights – when I made the choice to sleep with Daniel in his bed for that reason. At least that way I knew that he would get a good night's sleep, and – lying there next to him – so would I. In addition, it was important for Jimmy to get some rest since he had to work the following day. It was worth every minute to indulge Daniel and sleep with him all those nights, and I cherish the time I was able to do so. I just wish I hadn't lost my temper those other times while trying to get him to sleep.

On a few special occasions, we ended up with a family bed. One of my sweetest memories is of a night when Madi had come into our bed in the middle of the night, and I ended up going into Daniel's room to console him, as usual. He and I went through the whole feeding routine, and then he pointed his index finger towards our bedroom. Knowing that Madi was asleep in our bed, too, I told Daniel that we had to be very quiet.

I remember looking over at Jimmy, who had woken up, and having this overwhelming feeling of serenity as we looked at our two little monkeys sandwiched between us and sleeping so peacefully. We were a perfect family all squished together. Of course, Jimmy and I sacrificed *our* comfort and sleep to make sure they received theirs, but it was well worth every restless minute that night and all the yawns the next day.

Chapter Fourteen

SPRING

That Easter was such a special and memorable holiday for our family. Madi woke very early in anticipation of a visit from the Easter Bunny and simply couldn't wait to see what treats he'd brought for her and Daniel. The four of us went into the living room to discover all kinds of goodies. The sweetest part was that Madi was more excited about the festivities for Daniel's sake than for her own. She helped him dig through his Easter basket and gleefully showed him each and every gift he'd received. There's nothing like two happy kids on a sugar high before 7:00 a.m.! We spent the rest of the morning at Bubba and Grandpa's, where the kids received yet another welcome set of Easter baskets.

Jimmy took Daniel home for his nap around noon, while Madi and I headed over to our friend Ruby's house for a special Easter celebration. But since Daniel was missing the fun, Madi wasn't quite satisfied even though she enjoyed the Easter egg hunt. She and I decided that after the party, we would go home and create our own Easter egg hunt for Daniel.

We waited for the arrival of cousins Murphy and Myles to set up the egg hunt, and then they each helped one of the kids find the hidden eggs. Murphy walked around with Daniel, and it was so cute because it seemed as if Daniel wanted Murphy's approval to pick up an egg! Daniel would look down at the ground, point at an egg, and then look at him like, "Is it okay for me to pick it up?" He also refused to go anywhere in the yard that seemed "out of bounds" to him, especially if it looked like he might get dirty. In that case, Daniel would point and grunt to Murphy as if to say, "You get that one – I'm not going near that dirt!"

We had another sweet surprise on Easter Sunday – our fifteen-year old niece (and godchild), Kelsey, arrived unexpectedly from Michigan for a week's visit. It was a heartwarming reunion for Kelsey and Madi, and it was Kelsey's first time to meet her new cousin, Daniel. They hit it off instantly. Kelsey was very diplomatic about making sure that Madi, who adores her, was given equal time and attention. What Kelsey loved more than anything was how proudly Madi introduced Daniel as "her little brother." We had our first family dinner outing with both kids, along with Grandpa Murphy and Kelsey. It was a memorable (yet profoundly emotional) evening because we all felt that Grandma Pauline should have been there to enjoy all of the grandchildren together at last, especially at one of her favorite restaurants, no less.

The month of May brought many more fun "firsts" for Daniel. Thanks to the kindness of friends, Daniel – accompanied by his big sister – was treated to his first trip to Build-A-Bear. He was a bit overwhelmed by the experience, so Madi and I ended up choosing a bear for him once it became clear that he was confused with so many choices. Daniel loved the "stuffing station" and really enjoyed stomping the foot pedal to stuff his bear. Madi had a ball taking her brother around to the various stations and trying to engage him in the total experience. We made sure that his bear had a heart-beat, and Madi recorded the sweetest message, "I love you, Daniel," which he treasured. We planned to bring his bear – named *Lucky* – to the hospital with us so that Daniel would be able to hear Madi's recorded voice message over and over.

That week, the four of us took our first family trip to the beach. We opted for a late afternoon outing, complete with dinner for the kids as well as wine for Mommy and Daddy. Daniel was mesmerized by the vastness of the big, blue ocean, but he clearly felt more comfortable watching Madi splash in the waves from a distance. He rarely left Daddy's chair, and while he also didn't seem crazy about the sand, he did enjoy chasing some birds around.

I was frantic that day because the water was so wild. There were rip currents galore, and jellyfish were washed up all over the beach. Within minutes, Madi was yards down the shore, and I couldn't help myself from letting out a paranoid shriek from time to time, even though I knew she was in capable, safe hands with Jimmy.

As we were leaving the beach, I noticed a sign and pointed out to Jimmy, "Look, honey, the sign says: 'Saturday – rip currents and jellyfish'," to which Madi adamantly responded, "We better not come on Saturdays anymore. Fridays will be a much better day!"

After a couple of months, Madi and Daniel had really become close-knit siblings. I have the most joyous memory of looking in the back seat of the van one day – while stopped at a traffic light – and seeing the two of them holding hands from their individual car seats. It was so sweet to watch them smile at each other while they were swinging their arms in unison. I remember feeling so satisfied and complete – my heart absolutely overflowed with joy.

I will always cherish the memories of our favorite games together. Daniel loved it when I would do "This little piggy" with his toes. I know he didn't have a clue what any of it meant, but it was obviously fun for him anyway. He anticipated that final moment when I would tickle him, and then he would roll around squealing with delight.

Jimmy and I would pretend to fight over Daniel. I would hold him tightly and claim him as "my baby." Jimmy and I would go back and forth with him and me each pretending to argue over whose baby Daniel was. Daniel would clutch my neck so tightly, look at Jimmy, and say, "Mine!" as if he weren't willing to share me with Jimmy! I will always carry those precious moments with me.

Jimmy loved to chase the kids around the house, frequently walking as if he were Frankenstein with his arms straight out in front of him. Daniel would sometimes try to fake Jimmy out and walk like Frankenstein too, in an attempt to try to scare him back. It was a brilliant strategy! Daniel's monster walk soon became accompanied by a special expression, which we named his "scary face." I think Daniel started to believe that he could actually do damage with his evil eyes – probably because of the fantastic melodramatic reactions that we gave him!

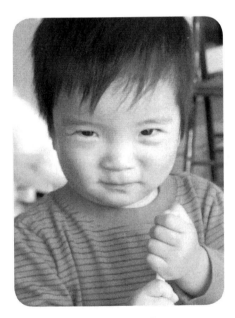

Daniel's "scary" face

COUNTDOWN TO SURGERY | May 5, 2010

As I write this post, I am looking at Daniel sound asleep in his stroller. I took him for a walk this morning and he promptly fell asleep. His nights have been so restless - filled with whimpers and cries. I know we can count on, at least once in the night, him crying out loud and tearing out of his bedroom. By the time I can get to him, he's already in the hallway. I do not think he's awake, but it does seem that he's looking for us, and he's clearly comforted once he finds us.

Last night, for the first time, he had run into Madi's room crying. I think he loves her companionship so much. If he had his wish, I know he'd sleep with her every night. He seems to be comfortable in his room and goes to sleep without much issue now, but the nights have been rough for him. Sorry for rambling, but I know that his nights are affecting his days and he's very tired. I am so relieved when he has a good nap.

It's hard to believe that this time next week, Daniel's heart surgery will have taken place and we will be on the road to his recovery. It seems like we've been talking about it for so long now. We are prepared that the next few weeks, months maybe, will not be easy for him or for us, but there's really no alternative here. We would appreciate your prayers for a successful surgery and for a speedy and full recovery.

That week, I called our church office (St. Vincent Ferrer) to add Daniel's name to the sick prayer list in the parish bulletin.

"Have you had Daniel anointed?" the kind woman on the phone (whom I came to know as Linda) gently asked. I had never really thought about it or even known that it was an option, so Linda graciously made an appointment for me to bring Daniel in the next week.

It is interesting to me now that Daniel and I were alone for this awesome blessing, in the truest sense of the words, and I believe that God planned it that way. We dropped Madi off at school that morning, headed for St. Vincent's, and Father Michael greeted us outside the church office. He was taken by surprise when Daniel exited the minivan wearing Madi's plastic pink high-heeled Barbie shoes! Daniel adored those shoes and loved wearing them because they belonged to his beloved big sister. I let him wear the Barbie shoes to drop Madi off at school that day, and – thankfully – Father Michael got a chuckle out of it. Daniel obviously "felt the love" and jumped right into Father Michael's arms.

I hadn't really known Father Michael before this experience, and I came to discover that he is a very kind and loving Priest with a great sense of humor. Father Michael, an older gentleman (and a very "fatherly" or "grandfatherly" figure) with silver hair and eyeglasses, is the huggable type – like a giant teddy bear. He is a fabulous Mass Celebrant, as well, and his passion for the Word would light up the sanctuary. Little did I know how special he would become to our family. Father Michael took to Daniel immediately – he just has that way with kids. It seemed that he felt especially connected to Daniel as he had adopted two sons of his own. We followed Father Michael into the church, after (of course) we removed the pink Barbie shoes from Daniel's feet.

The Sacrament of Anointing was heavenly. Daniel was so quiet – much calmer than usual. Father Michael laid him on the altar and rubbed a sacred holy oil (referred to as "chrism") on his forehead. He then offered Daniel up to our Lord, asking God to take our sweet son into his arms. After the anointing, Father Michael laid his hands on both of us, and prayed for our strength and for our protection. It was so peaceful in that sanctuary, and it was an experience that I will remember forever. Daniel and I were only there for about fifteen minutes, but it was the most spiritual and serene period of time, and the Sacrament felt completely filled with the power of the Holy Spirit.

When Father Michael finished the Sacrament of Anointing, he allowed Daniel to run all over the sanctuary, which made Daniel's day since I constantly had to peel him off the sanctuary steps every Sunday morning during the children's blessing at Mass! I remember – afterwards – wishing that I had known in advance how special Daniel's anointing of the sick would be. I felt like our entire family would have loved to be present for that special ritual. I am incredibly grateful to have had such a personal and treasured memory with my son.

Another precious memory for me was the way Madi would dress up her little brother. Daniel adored anything and everything that Madi did with (or to) him, including wearing her clothing and accessories. She would put him in her dresses, and he was in his glory. I remember one day in particular when we were caring for the cats of our neighbor and friend, Diane. I went to get the kids from Madi's room, and Daniel was wearing her denim dress. He was so pleased about it that I really didn't have the heart to make him change his clothes. As we crossed the street to fulfill our obligation, I hoped that none of the neighbors were out and about to question my motherly instincts! On that day, I got lucky.

Both Madi and Daniel loved to raid my closet together and parade around in my high-heeled shoes – I suppose someone should get some use out of them! Daniel also loved to have his fingernails painted. The first time this happened was at Bubba's house when she was painting Madi's nails. When Madi's nails were done, Daniel marched over and splayed his little fingers out, so Bubba went along with it and grabbed some clear polish. No go. Daniel grabbed the same pearl pink that Madi had chosen and indicated to Bubba that he much preferred that color! Daniel got his way, so his fingers and toes were painted with light pink – which is every Dad's nightmare, but Jimmy and I didn't care. As long as the kids were happy, we were happy.

Daniel's next manicure was even more comical. Hannah, the only person to babysit Daniel other than a grandparent, babysat the kids one night while Jimmy and I went out with friends. The next morning when Daniel woke up, we could see that his fingernails had been painted bright red. Madi told us that Daniel had picked out that color and Hannah had obliged. The funniest part was at Mass that morning when we sat next to a family with several young boys. As Daniel would try to move closer to them, the boys looked at him strangely and scooted away. It cracked me up because I could see them staring at his nails. Jimmy and I loved allowing Daniel to express himself, and we knew that he was only trying to mimic Madi. After all, he was only two years old! There was no harm done, and there would be plenty of time to teach him boy stuff – or so we thought.

That Wednesday, Jimmy, Madi and I took Daniel down to Miami for his pre-op testing at the hospital. It was a long and grueling day. We began the morning by meeting with the cardiothoracic surgeon and his nurse practitioner, who spent about an hour reviewing all of the details of the open-heart surgery. The surgical team had decided that the right procedure for Daniel's anatomy was called the Rastelli operation – used for a variety of congenital heart defects characterized by the same issues that Daniel had. He explained the details of the operation to us, and then he began to divulge the risks involved. Jimmy and I didn't want to *think* about risks – let alone *hear* about them.

I couldn't help but ask, "Can we just *not do* the surgery?"

The surgeon firmly replied, "I'm sorry, but there really isn't an option here."

So after signing what seemed like one hundred consent forms, the nurse practitioner led us to another room for Daniel's echocardiogram, which went rather smoothly but took several hours. Then we moved on to chest x-rays, which is when they determined (unbeknownst to us) that damage had been done to Daniel's lung as a result of poor oxygen saturation, and the lower right lobe of his lung was compromised. The blood work, however, was unquestionably the worst part of our day. The nurses – once again – weren't able to find Daniel's veins in his arms or hands, so they finally resorted to taking blood from the tops of his feet. Madi and I had gone to get a snack while Jimmy and Daniel waited for his turn.

When Madi and I came back, we realized that the boys had been called into one of the exam rooms because we could hear Daniel's blood-curdling screams from down the hallway. We hurried into the room to find Daniel being held down by four nurses, with Jimmy by his side attempting to console him. When Madi and I entered the room, I was utterly paralyzed at the sight, and – as if I were stuck in ten inches of quicksand – could barely move a muscle. Jimmy was completely overwrought and yelled at me to please get Madi out of the room.

Instinctively, I ran to Daniel's side to console him. It seemed like a good time to switch roles, so Jimmy hustled Madi back out to the waiting room and calmed her down. Our poor little son had endured so much agony, yet he had a smile on his face just ten minutes later. It had been an entire day filled with testing, poking, and pain, and all four of us were mentally wiped out. We drove home from Miami very relieved that the day was over. Unfortunately, it was only a taste of what was to come.

Jimmy and I allowed our son to get away with a little more than usual that week. Daniel loved to be in Madi's bedroom, but she would only rarely allow him to come in and feel totally welcome. He loved everything about her room – her toys, her bed, her collectibles. Madi would go berserk for fear that Daniel would break something in there, and she would usually try to coax him back into his room where they would then play beautifully together.

Daniel never quite understood what the big deal was about. He wanted nothing more than to be together in Madi's room playing with all of her beautiful, frilly girl things, and I know he would have done anything to share that bed with her! A few mornings that week (while Madi was in school), Daniel and I went into her room and played on her bed long enough to satisfy his curiosity. It was such a treat for him, and he was totally overjoyed pretending that her beautiful purple bed belonged to him, too.

Madi's baby doll

The kids played together so nicely that week. One afternoon, I could hear the two of them giggling in the bathroom for quite a while. I went to check on them and found Daniel sitting on the toilet – while Madi was teaching him how to cut with scissors! What a sight! There were tatters of colored construction paper all over the floor. Daniel was in his glory, and Madi was so pleased that she was such a good instructor! They were so happy and cute together that I couldn't possibly interrupt their "moment," so I allowed them to proceed with their activity for about five more minutes before I finally decided it was time to get Daniel – and the scissors – off the toilet!

I felt rather blessed to spend Mother's Day with both of my beautiful children, but truthfully – since the holiday took place just two days before Daniel's surgery – Mother's Day was really a blur to me that year. Sadly, instead of fully embracing my special day with my son as I should have, I worried the day away while we packed and planned for our departure the next afternoon.

Chapter Fifteen

PREPARING FOR SURGERY

Jimmy and I left the house on May 10th feeling uneasy in our hearts about Daniel's surgery. Even though we were hopeful, faithful, and confident of a positive outcome, a parent can't help but feel uneasy before a medical procedure. Bubba and Grandpa moved into our house that day, and as they said goodbye to Daniel, I had to push back thoughts that it could possibly be the last time they would see him. I still don't know why I felt that way, but I did. Jimmy felt that way too, but we never admitted it to each other until much later. It was so hard to leave Madi, but my husband and I stayed upbeat about the situation and talked about all the fun things we would do together when we got back.

Madi had allowed Daniel to pick out one of her stuffed animals to take with him. Of her myriad of animals, Daniel chose a little pink bear named "Baby Girl." He adored "Baby Girl." He would smile adoringly at it and kiss his sister's bear with his little air-filled cheeks. He loved it because it belonged to Madi.

Grandpa Murphy decided to meet us in Miami and spend the night so that we could all go to the hospital together in the morning. Jimmy and I still can't put our finger on it, but there was something notably different about Daniel that night. He walked through the hotel with a different air about him, and our son was more confident than we had ever seen him. Not since China had the four of us been alone together, and it felt somewhat strange and surreal.

We had planned to have dinner at the hotel restaurant, but something inside told me that we should venture out somewhere else – somewhere away from the hotel. We consulted with the concierge, and he recommended a great Spanish seafood restaurant on the Intracoastal Waterway. That was the best place he could have ever recommended. Daniel was fascinated by both the boats in the canal and the airplanes arriving and departing through the Miami skies. He was intrigued by just about everything because it was all a new experience for him. Daniel pointed his little index finger like crazy, inquisitively soaking up every single sight.

Dinner at Casablanca

We had been instructed to bathe Daniel with an antibacterial soap (given to us at pre-op) to cleanse him for the surgery. When we returned to the hotel that night, we followed our instructions, but Daniel fought it as though he felt something was wrong. Maybe he just sensed our fear, or perhaps he just didn't like the smell of that yucky stuff. Jimmy and I both felt so uneasy about his actions and how he writhed about as we sponge-bathed him. At that point, Jimmy and I wished that – more than anything else – we could just get in our car with Daniel and drive far, far away, but we knew that his surgery had to be done.

The next morning, Jimmy and I woke up early to take our showers before we woke Daniel. Our son had slept fairly well the night before, probably better than we had. We drove over to the hospital, parked the car in the parking garage, and walked over to the Children's Hospital. We took the elevator up to the 5th Floor and headed to the P.I.R.R. (Patient Intake and Recovery Room). We were all too familiar with our surroundings, but Daniel did not seem even a bit frightened, which surprised us. Although his trips down to Miami had resulted in so much pain and agony, our son was not fearful. He was the same sweet, special little boy that he always was.

The nurses checked Daniel in, and we put his little hospital gown on him. This time, they knew better than to give him any juice. Administering Daniel's IV was easier this time too – thank God – since they chose to give him some sedation first. The anesthesiologists, Jimmy and Amanda, came in to greet Daniel. He was all smiles, as were they. He had felt their warmth the first time we'd met them in March (for his catheter procedure), and it was obvious that our son could feel their warmth again. Dr. Amanda (the anesthesiologist) gave Daniel his little cup of sleepy, and he drank it all down without a fuss.

Daniel was always so good at taking medicines, and within fifteen minutes or so, we could see that the sedation was taking effect. Amanda was there at Daniel's bedside playing with him, engaging him, and trying to make sure he was comfortable for what was about to happen. We could tell that she was a very special person just by the way she handled our little boy and the other children we'd seen her interact with. Daddy had been teasing Daniel with "Baby Girl." He would wave the little pink bear in Daniel's face and would then pull it away. All of a sudden, Daniel grabbed "Baby Girl" from Jimmy and very seriously admonished him in what must have been Chinese, because it certainly didn't sound like English! The look on his face was priceless, and he sternly waved a finger at Daddy. Daniel then handed the bear to Amanda, and – just like that – he was happy again. I think that might have been the moment when Amanda fell in love with our baby.

About twenty minutes later, everything was set up and ready to go. We agreed that Daniel was a mean little drunk, and chuckled together about his grumpy behavior. The nurses and doctors allowed us to walk his gurney down to the surgical area and say our pre-op good-byes to Daniel there. We did not, of course, realize that they truly would be goodbyes from Daniel as we knew him. My husband and I had faith that this precious child of God would be safe. We hugged him tightly and kissed his face, but even though we trusted he was in good hands, Jimmy and I couldn't help the tears from falling.

Amanda wheeled Daniel into the surgical prep area, and what we later found out (from speaking with various medical team members) was how sweet Daniel was in the operating room. As they waited for his sedation to take full effect, Amanda introduced him to every member of the surgical team, and Daniel happily waved, smiled, and said hello to everyone. Grandpa, Jimmy, and I headed to the waiting area, knowing full well that it was going to be a very long day. We were told that the surgery would take seven to eight hours, so we were mentally prepared for a full day of "pray and wait."

A few hours into the surgery – probably due to stress – I started having major pains in my abdomen that just wouldn't subside (even after an hour or so). I hoped maybe there was a clinic in the hospital, and perhaps I could just run in and quickly see a doctor. Apparently, there was no speedy clinic around, but the emergency room was located on the ground floor of our building. Hey, I had time to kill, why not try, right? I realized – as I was sitting in the primary E.R. of Miami – that I felt like I was right in the middle of one of those popular hospital T.V. shows.

I sat in the waiting room for well over an hour before I was finally sent to a preliminary nurses' station. I explained my situation, and after further questioning, they sent me to a second waiting room in another area of the hospital. I was on hour number three when I noticed that the pain had drastically subsided. Was it my imagination that I felt 100% better? No, it wasn't. All of a sudden, panic set in that my son was having major heart surgery upstairs, and here I was stuck in an emergency waiting room over absolutely nothing! I scurried over to the nurses' station, told them that I felt better, explained the situation upstairs with Daniel, and they – thankfully – allowed me to leave. What I would later find out is that I had, for the first time in my life, suffered from the rupturing of acute endometrial cysts.

When I got back upstairs, the guys were still waiting but had received updates that the surgery was going well. With that welcome news, Jimmy and I decided that it would be a good time to walk over to the Ronald McDonald house to check in and unload our luggage. The manager kindly showed us to our room and gave us a quick tour of the facilities. He also assigned us our 'house chores' of cleaning the common kitchen counters and cabinets on a daily basis. Jimmy and I were thankful to have a place to rest our heads, but we really hadn't planned on staying in Miami for very long. We quickly unpacked our belongings and rushed back to the hospital.

Finally, at around 4:00 p.m., the surgeon came into the waiting room and reported that Daniel was out of surgery and that it had been completely successful. Daniel's body appeared to be stable and strong, and they expected him to be out of the hospital within days. All three of us were obviously elated and fought back tears of relief as we received that blessed news. I took two pictures of our son that night, but I instinctively knew – from the very second that camera snapped – that those photos were not to be shared. I can only explain that something inside, or the Holy Spirit perhaps, told me that they were private, sacred, and for our eyes only. We never showed them to anyone.

BYE BYE BLUE BABY | May 11, 2010

We never noticed just how blue Daniel's little fingernails and toenails were...until now. Now his little nail beds are the most beautiful shade of pink! We swear his skin tone is noticeably different too. It's amazing.

Our little baby is truly a fighter. They were able to remove his breathing tube at around 6:00 this evening. It is painfully obvious that he detests restraints, so the plethora of tubes coming out of him are driving him crazy already! He goes wild just about every hour on the hour, and we are being told that the next 12 - 18 hours will be the roughest. It will be a delicate balancing act of managing his pain and making sure that he's breathing properly with his new plumbing.

Jimmy and I decided that we should both stay in the P.I.C.U. room for now. That way one of us can rest and the other can be next to Daniel during the night. We both feel that someone should be next to him at all times right now. Thank you all so much for your prayers. They mean the world to us, and they are obviously working! Will update tomorrow...

Chapter Sixteen

THE TURNING POINT

If only we had known on that night what we would learn in the three weeks to follow. When Daniel came out of his surgery, he appeared so strong that the doctors predicted he'd be home in days. He had only been in his P.I.C.U. room for about an hour when he began coming out of the anesthesia and attempted to get up on all fours. Daniel seemed to be doing so well that, at around 6 p.m., the attending physician in charge of the floor that evening made the call to extubate him. There was every indication that Daniel was ready for the breathing tube to come out, so they removed it, and he seemed to do fine – at first.

Jimmy and I both decided to stay in the hospital room with our little boy that night, and we took turns napping in a chair that converted to a bed. Today my heart is filled with regret that I slept for even one solitary minute. Had my body not failed me earlier – which had resulted in major exhaustion – I might have tried harder to stay awake all night. Through the course of the night, we watched Daniel's condition slowly decline without realizing the severity of his situation. Through the hours, we watched his blood oxygen levels (on the monitors) slowly move downwards from 100% saturation into the eighties. Initially, neither we – nor his nurses – were alarmed because Daniel's body was accustomed to lower blood oxygen saturation levels (in the seventies). But point by point, his numbers continued to drop.

The nurses ran hourly blood gas tests on Daniel, but the results were not alarming. Through the course of the night, however, his breathing became more labored. Apparently, all the craziest and scariest things happened while I was sleeping. In an effort to assist Daniel's breathing, the nurses first placed a ventilator over his nose, and then they ended up putting an oxygen mask on him, but he still struggled to breathe. I'll never forget the moaning sounds that came out of our baby as he gasped for breath, but Jimmy and I were just so damn ignorant. We simply had no idea what was happening inside that little body.

At approximately 3:00 a.m., a chest x-ray was taken in order to make sure that everything still looked okay; it detected some fluid in his lungs – but, apparently, nothing alarming. The cardiothoracic surgeon later explained that a reasonable amount of fluid is normal after surgery since Daniel's lungs were being forced to adapt to a new and fully performing heart. But those organ functions usually tend to balance out as the lungs learn to do their new job effectively. Once again – the physicians weren't alarmed.

The nurses began to get nervous at around 6:00 a.m. – just after I had fallen asleep in the chair for one last nap. Daniel's blood gas levels had crept up to an abnormal range, and he still struggled to breathe. That was about the time when things really took a turn for the worst.

At 8:00 a.m., I woke up abruptly to the bone-chilling sounds of incessant hospital-trauma beeping. The bright, overhead fluorescent lights flooded Daniel's room, and there was obvious commotion as six or more doctors were crowded around his bedside. I had no idea what was happening, but I was awake enough to realize that something had gone terribly wrong.

I jumped up from the chair in the corner where I had been lying, and then ducked down and peered between all of the medical equipment to look for Jimmy. I caught a glimpse of him outside the room, and my heart plummeted when I read my husband's body language. He was pacing back and forth, running both his hands through his hair, and he had tears in his eyes. I knew it wasn't good. Trying not to disturb the medical staff, I escaped from the room and ran to Jimmy. I barely understood what he was saying. It was as if I could see his lips moving, but I was unable to process his words.

"Daniel went into cardiac arrest," I heard my husband say. And those two words – cardiac arrest – would change our lives forever.

Jimmy hadn't wanted to wake me when Daniel's condition began to rapidly decline. After his last blood gas test came back with unsatisfactory levels, the doctors decided that they needed to put Daniel's breathing tube back in. But when they attempted to do this, Daniel vomited. The lactic acid in his system, along with his respiratory distress, had thrown him into cardiac arrest. Thank God the amazing on-duty nurse, Kim, was right next to Daniel when his heart stopped, and she did not miss one beat. She continued to give him manual CPR until the crash cart was brought into the room moments later.

Jimmy and I were in a state of shock, and neither of us was able to comprehend what was happening. We did not want to get in the staff's way, so we scurried into the empty patient room next to Daniel's, and silently watched through the window as tragedy unfolded before our eyes. This painful scenario wasn't part of our plan.

After what seemed like an eternity – but was probably about five minutes in total – the floor nurse approached us and suggested that we go to the P.I.C.U. waiting room on the floor. She promised us that they would keep us informed. The amazing part was the timing. Since Daniel's cardiac arrest happened at 8:00 a.m., and shift change had taken place at 7:00 a.m., all of the necessary surgeons, anesthesiologists, and medical personnel were there to act immediately. We watched them, one by one, run off the elevator and enter the P.I.C.U. As each of them made eye contact with Jimmy and me, we could see the anguish in their faces. We could practically feel the pain that they felt for us. Daniel had quickly become one of their favorite patients.

After about twenty minutes of pure shock, the surgeon's assistant came and found us in the waiting room.

"The good news is that Daniel is still with us," she said.

"*Still with us?*" I said to myself.

Anger began to swell inside me like a tsunami as those words echoed in my head. We were obviously relieved that our son was still alive, but we were stunned that this was truly happening. At that point, I was in total denial that an alternative to life even existed for our son. Jimmy and I came to the stark realization of just how grave Daniel's condition was – and we felt totally betrayed. It felt like such a slap in the face because we had put so much faith in those doctors, and we both were convinced that Daniel would walk out of that hospital within days. How could this possibly happen when he'd been doing so well just the night before?

The assistant explained that they needed to put Daniel on a special machine, called an ECMO machine (extracorporeal membrane oxygenation), to assist his heart and lungs. But when they attempted to hook him up, they discovered an open artery that was stealing blood from the machine and not allowing it to do its job sufficiently. They needed our approval to perform an emergency catheterization procedure to locate and cap the artery. In our minds, we had no choice but to expeditiously go along with this plan, so – once again – we placed our son's fate in God's hands and gave them the approval to proceed.

As we called our family and friends to report Daniel's major setback, Jimmy and I were still stunned beyond belief. The truth is, we still hadn't totally grasped what had happened. Grandpa Murphy was the first to show up at the hospital, followed by Matt, and then our friend Lisa. I had asked Lisa to bring me a rosary; she brought two. The day seemed like such a blur – it was so surreal, and we had nothing to do but anxiously wait, and beg the Lord for our son's life.

After several hours, the catheterization nurse came out to let us know that they were almost done, and they had successfully capped the artery. At that time, Jimmy and I didn't fully comprehend what that meant, but we felt like it was a medical Hail Mary pass, especially since the nurse was smiling. We had thought that this (now-capped) artery had been responsible for the bleeding in his lungs, and we thought this procedure would fix Daniel. What my husband and I failed to realize was that they needed to cap the artery for the heart and lung machine to work effectively and sustain our son's organ function.

When the Director of Catheterization finally came to speak with us, she did not look quite as thrilled as her head nurse had. Yes, they had managed to cap the artery and stop the bleeding, but it was evident that she was not pleased with the situation. She did not give us the positive feedback – the warm and fuzzy feeling – that we were looking for, and that we so desperately *wanted to hear*. She told us that Daniel would be wheeled back to his room soon, and that they would let us know as soon as we could see him.

As we impatiently waited for that to happen, I caught a glimpse of her inside the P.I.C.U. area venting to several members of her medical team. It was obvious that she was furious with something or someone. When she saw me standing there, I could've sworn I saw her angrily mouth the words, "There's the mother now!" and then she stormed off down the hall. This particular surgeon, who is known for **not** being warm and fuzzy, was visibly upset about Daniel's condition, and I knew in my heart that something wasn't right.

After what seemed like an eternity, we were finally allowed to see our baby. His chest was now open, which – though it sounds horrifying to think about (and it was painful to see) – can be common procedure when swelling occurs, or if the medical team needs quick access to the organs. In Daniel's case, they needed to monitor his heart very carefully. When I say that his chest was "open" it means that they had only covered the surface area with a thin, clear protective film in order to avoid infection.

Jimmy and I would not be able to hold our baby and give him the physical affection that we wanted so desperately to give. We were slapped with the stark new reality that we needed to "suit up" before entering our son's room. We were informed that gowns, facemasks and gloves were now mandatory; we would have worn armor if we needed to – it didn't matter to us. All we wanted was to see our little boy walk out of that hospital.

UPDATE ON OUR SWEET LITTLE FIGHTER | May 12, 2010

I don't have to tell you how concerned we are right now. It is so hard to be away from his bedside, but the doctors really believe it's in our best interest to get some rest, for our sake – for Daniel's sake. We know you are all with us, and we have received so many beautiful emails and comments. Thank you so much. They keep us going, and remind us that we must keep the faith, even during this most difficult of times. They have also required us to have lots of Kleenex on hand.

When we left the hospital this evening, Daniel was stable. His heart is working, and the ECMO machine is doing the heavy lifting to give his heart a rest. The good news we have to hang onto: his body is producing urine, which it wasn't producing much last night. Though his heart is beating slowly, it is indeed beating. His oxygen level is stable. He is a fighter. The anesthesiologists, who have come to love Daniel dearly, gave us reassurance that he was even fighting under sedation and he moved all of his limbs, which is good.

The next steps: they will continue to allow his heart to get stronger, while he remains on the ECMO machine. They will work on building up his lung capacity again, and we can only take things day by day. The surgeon was "cautiously optimistic."

We can't thank you enough for your love and support. Please continue spreading the word to all of your prayer chains. We are so blessed to have so many people who care about Daniel. We will update in the morning.

That evening, the hospital staff urged us to return to the Ronald McDonald House to get some rest. They knew we were exhausted and, as much as Jimmy and I wanted to stay at the hospital, we did believe that Daniel would be better off with well-rested parents. The staff assured us that our son was in good hands. They promised to call us with any developments, and we were welcome to call at any time to check on him.

My husband and I knew that sleep was imperative for us in the long haul, so we took their advice and headed back to the Ronald McDonald House. For obvious reasons, however, it was difficult to sleep. As we cuddled together and held each other tightly in one of our room's twin-size beds, we both broke down in tears as the severity of the situation, and the uncertainty of our son's fate, began to sink in.

Chapter Seventeen

CRITICAL CARE

The day after Daniel's cardiac arrest, Jimmy and I began to attend daily Catholic Mass at the hospital's chapel. Those Masses provided us with so much peace and hope. The homily of the first Mass we attended was about using our God-given talents to spread the message of God's word and his steadfast love for us. Since I don't believe in coincidences, it was crystal clear to me that I should use our blog to spread His message of faith in our crisis.

In retrospect, I am amazed at what a profound impact Daniel's story began to have on people. Our son was included in prayer chains all over the country – even all over the world. People began uniting in faith, praying together for this little boy – this little fighter whose survival was against all odds. It was truly breath-taking to think how our Little Lamb of God affected so many people.

UPDATE ON DANIEL | May 13, 2010

Once again we are so humbled by all of the prayer warriors out there for Daniel. It sounds like the whole world must be praying for him. The morning brings us the following updates. On the good side, his organs seem to be stable. Though he is assisted by the ECMO machine, his heart beats are still stable. The obstacle today is Daniel's lung function. One of the necessary elements of the ECMO machine is Heparin, which is a blood thinner. Unfortunately, Heparin can cause bleeding. Daniel's lungs, for some reason, are filling with fluid from this and the various other medications he is on to reduce his swelling and increase urine output. Today is about trying to find out why his lungs are filling up and to try to make room for air so Daniel can breathe properly. We remain strong and we refuse to give up hope. We can clearly see that none of our friends and family are giving up either! He is such a strong little boy. We truly believe that God sent us halfway around the world to bring him home for a reason. We believe that reason is to be here with us. Please keep praying...

May 13th left us with some positive developments. That morning, we were joined at the hospital by Bubba and Grandpa along with Grandpa Murphy. Oh, the blessed comfort of having parents to be there for you, especially in such serious times of need. Jimmy and I saw more smiling faces in the intensive care unit throughout that day, and ours were included among them. We were cautioned that this would be a long road and there would be some steps backwards, but there was still hope and we needed to be very, very patient. My husband and I were thankful for the slightest of improvements as our little guy continued to hang in there and fight.

Daniel's heart rate and oxygen levels were stable. They began to wean him from the ECMO machine at a very slow pace, but the system was doing its job thus far. The drainage from suctioning Daniel's nose and mouth seemed to lessen a bit, and the doctors were seeing an improvement. Daniel also had less fluid coming from his lungs, so they were hopeful that what they were doing was working. Jimmy and I would find out, for sure, in the form of an x-ray the next morning. The staff had located a nebulizer treatment for Daniel's lungs that could be used without removing his ventilator, which would make the suctioning process much easier and more effective. They had also put Daniel on TPN (Total Parenteral Nutrition), which fed him intravenously and bypassed the process of eating and digestion.

When Jimmy and I walked into intensive care the morning of May 14th, Daniel had fared well through the night, and our relief brought tears of joy. His urine output had increased, and the nurses were able to lessen some of his medications. They'd weaned him a bit more from the ECMO machine during the night, and his heart was holding strong with the rest it had been given. We were told that the x-ray of his lungs was still pretty cloudy, but it did look slightly better than it had the day before. The medical staff seemed to be breathing a little easier when they visited Daniel's room that morning, too. Again – we were prepared for a long haul, but sweet Jesus it was such a relief to receive good news about our baby boy.

When Daniel's surgeon stopped by during rounds that morning, he confirmed that the fluid was lessening in Daniel's lungs, and they believed the bleeding had stopped. The cloudiness on the x-ray (which appeared to be blood) would take time to break down and filter out of his body. Additionally, Daniel was having some issues with liver and kidney function, but we were told that this was nothing unexpected for a patient who had gone through the trauma of cardiac arrest. As the surgeon explained these developments, he reminded us of the ups and downs we would experience along Daniel's road to recovery.

Daniel was still paralyzed in a medically-induced coma – on full sedation – for his safety, but we were told he could feel our touch, so we began to spend even more time at his bedside since he was in more stable condition. We brought his musical seahorse (named "Glowy" by Madi) to the hospital for him that evening, and his nurse was kind enough to put the sound on for him throughout the night. We figured the soft lullabies would soothe our baby, and that this would bring some familiarity from home, as well.

The medical care our son received was amazing to us. I would love to know how many millions of dollars worth of medical equipment sat inside that room. It was like a compound outside of his room, too. Daniel was hooked up to so many machines, in fact, that it was nearly impossible to access the private bathroom because of the wires and medical equipment. Daniel had two dedicated nurses every day, along with a charge nurse to supervise.

One of our favorite nurses was Angela, whom I dubbed our "angel," and she was so in tune with the children. She wouldn't touch Daniel without sweetly talking to him and letting him know exactly what she was doing to him. We loved her way of caring for him. She stressed the importance of music for Daniel, and helped us locate a CD player in the hospital's child life department to place in his room. Angela stressed the importance of keeping Daniel on a schedule so he would continue to recognize night from day. Jimmy and I began to play familiar cartoons on the television, like Curious George, and other morning favorites during the day and we read stories to him regularly. We would end the day by playing soft music, followed by his musical seahorse in hopes that it would help to keep him on a routine.

Angela also stressed the importance of touching and talking to Daniel. After his cardiac arrest, Jimmy and I almost treated our son as if he were sleeping, because that's how it seemed. It was difficult to comprehend that Daniel might actually be able to hear us and feel our touch since he was so heavily sedated in a medically-induced coma. Angela even recommended that we ignore the hospital proto-col and remove our latex gloves so that Daniel could feel Mommy and Daddy's skin touching his.

Angela gave us so much good advice, all of which really helped us maximize the closeness with our son despite the challenging cir-cumstances. Neither Jimmy nor I had ever been through something like this before, and we just didn't know what was right, what was wrong, or for that matter what was appropriate. Angela cleared up a lot of those confusing questions for us. It was obvious that – given her caring and gentle nature – she was a very good mother her-self. Based on how they cared for Daniel, it became easy to deter-mine which nurses were mothers and which were not. Don't get me wrong – they were all wonderful (and certainly capable) nurses, but some of them went that "extra mile" in a nurturing way, as only a good mother would instinctively know how to do.

At least twice each day, a team of about six doctors were camped outside of Daniel's room discussing action plans for the day. A spe-cialist, called a profusionist, was dedicated 24/7 to observe our son's blood and oxygen flow through the ECMO machine. Our family came to know each of these ECMO specialists so well. After all, we had plenty of time to converse with them. Respiratory special-ists came by several times daily to monitor Daniel's lung function and suction the fluids from his lungs and throat. And on several occasions, the neurology team came by to see if Daniel's brain function could be assessed. In his condition, it was far too diffi-cult to tell if his brain function had been compromised (since he was still fully sedated), so the neurology team opted to wait. They were also strongly encouraged to wait by Daniel's primary medical attendants since it wouldn't make much sense to put him through a neurological evaluation until his other organ issues had straightened themselves out.

We embraced the opportunity to meet with Daniel's surgeon every morning during rounds. We made sure we were at the hospital every morning by 7:00 a.m. for shift change. There was only one morning that we had inadvertently slept in and ran late by half an hour. Daniel's surgeon joked that he was about to call the Department of Children and Families on us.

Arriving at shift change gave Jimmy and me the opportunity to find out firsthand about Daniel's night from the nurse who was checking out. It also gave us a chance to greet the nurse who would be caring for him that day. I remember how we woke up with that nervous feeling each morning – sick to our stomachs until we arrived at the hospital to see our baby. Taking a shower each morning seemed like such a time-consuming chore, though we knew it would help us feel somewhat energized. I still can remember – as if it were only yesterday – being in that shower stall at the Ronald McDonald House, using lukewarm water to get clean; going through the motions with my stomach in knots. I recall the scent of the shampoo, and I prayed for good news each morning as I anxiously tried to scrub off the grief. It was nearly ninety degrees outside, yet my body shivered from nervousness as if it were snowing.

The walk from the Ronald McDonald House to the hospital seemed never-ending. Our hearts pounded as Jimmy and I would silently walk through the mile-long corridor – it seemed that long anyway – to reach the light at the other end. We would frequently make a quick pit-stop at Au Bon Pain to grab a quick coffee and bring something with us to eat – if we thought we could manage to eat that morning. Most times, we opted to go straight to the hospital to say good morning to Daniel. Once we checked in, saw our baby and caught our breath, then one of us could comfortably venture out for coffee. It totally depended on the day and on our emotions that morning.

There were two elevators in the building, but since one of them was almost always broken, going up to the 5th floor seemed to take forever and a day. Jimmy and I would desperately try to remain calm as we watched the numbers illuminate slowly from floor to floor, holding our breath as it finally approached the ground floor. Once we reached the 5th floor, entering the P.I.C.U. was always frightening for both Jimmy and me because we always wondered what we would encounter. We knew that if our night went without a phone call, that was a good thing – but it seemed only natural to develop that nervous knot in our stomachs as we turned the corner towards Room 25.

Since Daniel's room was filled with so much machinery and it was difficult to maneuver inside the room, Jimmy and I would usually set up camp just outside the door where we could watch our son's every move and observe everything that took place in his room. It seemed like the two of us would pretty much take over the immediate area, but the nurses and doctors were always so kind, and they never failed to offer up a chair if we needed one. They allowed us to pull up to the nurses' station so that Jimmy could begin his work (making his sales calls for the day), and I could write a blog post and check emails of friends for daily inspiration. Then my husband and I would take turns sitting by our son's bedside. We remained there all day long to monitor Daniel's progress, and took an occasional break to stretch or grab a bite to eat with friends or family.

Every machine in Daniel's room made a different sound, and we came to know the slightest difference of the beeping all too well. It's crazy how addictive observing those monitors can become. In an instant, those machines could literally send us from a state of serene peacefulness to a state of sheer panic. By the end of each day, our eyes were strained from staring at the lighted panels all day long, and both Jimmy and I were mentally exhausted from the stress of the situation altogether.

We usually left the hospital to eat dinner around five o'clock so we would have time to return to the hospital for the evening shift change. Seeing who would care for Daniel that night gave us the comfort level that we needed in order to sleep soundly – or attempt to, anyway. Jimmy and I became regulars at the local hotel patio bar, which was across the street only walking distance away. It became the main place where we could escape for an hour in the evening to have a cold beer, get some fresh air, and just decompress together at the end of our day. We were often joined by a family member or friends with whom we could discuss the details of the day and review Daniel's prognosis.

There were some nights that my husband and I joyously celebrated small victories, and there were other nights when we'd lost our appetites altogether. Sometimes, I felt that since our son couldn't eat, why in the world should we be able to sit there and enjoy a meal?

During our time at the hospital, our family was so blessed by the goodness of friends and family who delivered the most delicious baked goods for us and the hospital staff to enjoy. Naturally, the staff loved everything about our support system, and they could clearly see how blessed we were. It was such a fine example of the goodness of people coming together in a time of need.

We received a sweet message from Madi that day that obviously brought tears to our eyes:

Dear Daniel,

I love you, Daniel. I love you a little more than mommy
and daddy. I love you more than the whole world, Daniel,
because I know you are my little brother and you are going
to have heart surgery. When you get better you can jump off
the slide with daddy helping you like me. Daniel, yay, yay, yay.
Daniel James Murphy. When you come home I will let you
into my room. You can go wherever you want to because you
are my baby brother. I love you, Daniel. End it right now.

Dear Mommy and Daddy,

I love you mommy and daddy so much. I'm using my kissing
hand. I hope you are using your kissing hand too. Mommy,
hug Daniel for me. I hope you kiss Daniel's bear for me,
okay? I wish I could be with Daniel. I made a card for Daniel
but I cannot find it. I will make another one, okay?
Mommy can you send a note for us too please? Done.

Chapter Eighteen

FAITH

"Glory, glory, hallelujah! Glory, glory, hallelujah!
Glory, glory, hallelujah! His truth is marching on."

That chorus echoed in my head constantly – and I mean *constantly* – throughout the days and nights to come. It gave me strength when I felt weak, and it provided me with peace when I felt unsettled. At the time, I had no idea how or why that song had popped into my head or what all the song's lyrics were, but as I reflect on the verses today, I find it simply amazing that the Holy Spirit filled my head with that song, which I've included in the Appendix.

On May 15th, Daniel's lung x-ray had again improved. It was not drastic and it would still be a slow process, but the x-ray definitely looked as if he were getting better. We had been praying that the weekend would bring lots of healing for Daniel's body so that they could begin to further wean him from the ECMO machine because, apparently, it is not good for the body to remain on the machine for too long. Daniel's kidney and liver function were being monitored carefully and – like his progress in general – seemed to be moving in the right direction. The kindness and words of inspiration from friends and family were now keeping us going every day and every moment. Jimmy and I felt blessed that Sherril's sister-in-law, Kim, was a nurse at Mass General in Boston and worked very closely with their pediatric cardiology team. With every stumbling block we faced, Kim was able to educate us about each obstacle and provide us with insight about Daniel's treatment that helped us sleep at night. We breathed a sigh of relief that evening as our baby's progress continued to slowly improve.

The next day, Bubba and Grandpa came to sit with Daniel while we drove home to spend time with Madi. Though we hated to leave, it did feel good to physically get away, and it felt right that family members were there to spend time with Daniel in our absence. It was such a blessing to have my mom and dad around. Madi sent Bubba to the hospital with her biggest Mother Goose Nursery Rhyme book to read to Daniel.

Madi was truly upset that, because of her age, she wasn't allowed to come up and see Daniel. We empathized with her, but knew it would be too upsetting for her to see him the way he was. His sweet little face was contorted from tape and tubes. Daniel was hooked up to a web of lines and/or machines, and his eyes were usually covered with gauze. When they weren't covered, his eyes were filled with lubricant to keep them from drying out since he always slept with his eyelids slightly open. It was not the way we wanted her to see her little brother.

Bubba and Grandpa set up camp outside the P.I.C.U. room as we had, and we drove – with Madi – back home to spend time together. It gave us a chance to remember what "home" looked like, do some laundry, grab a bite to eat, and play a game or two with Madi. After a couple of hours – which always flew by – we would pack up the car and drive back down to Miami. Since the hospital was far, it gave Jimmy and me a good chance to catch up with our daughter and have precious conversation with her.

That day of our trip back home, the profusionists had continued to wean Daniel off the ECMO machine and – fortunately – his body seemed to be responding well. Our son's x-rays continued to look good, and we hoped that every day would bring more room for air flow into his lungs. They had started giving him a small amount of formula through a nose tube so his body wouldn't 'forget' how to process food. Daniel was looking a little bit more like himself every day.

A Blessed Sunday | May 16, 2010

Sunday feels so important today. A day of rest, a day of prayer, a day of our Lord. We can only imagine the prayers going out to Daniel today. So many of you have added him to prayer lists, dedicated Masses in his name, and simply prayed for him – which is the most we could ever ask for. Thank you so much.

We haven't seen his x-ray yet this morning, but hear that his lungs are improving. We will ask to see it this morning. Our issue of the moment seems to be his kidneys. There are certain levels of things that are elevating, and he is on "watch" by the doctors. We pray that these levels balance out before they become a problem. It's a watch and wait scenario. Other than that, Daniel is stable. They are actually planning on weaning him more from the ECMO machine today. He is proving to be so strong. We can hardly wait for the day we carry his sweet little booty out of here. Happy Sunday. Praise the Lord!

Sherril had been down to visit on Sunday afternoon, and that night as we left the hospital (just after shift change), she and I were feeling a bit uncomfortable. I had just finished explaining to Sherril how unsettling it was to be unfamiliar with the night nurses and doctors who – since they operated in three-day shifts – hadn't cared for Daniel before. Just as we finished our conversation, the elevator doors opened for us to exit the 5th floor. Sherril and I were greeted on the elevator by a female chaplain, who introduced herself to us as Reverend Mary.

Without having heard a word of our conversation, Reverend Mary proceeded to tell us how wonderful the night nurses were, especially the Sunday night staff. From God's ears to her lips! Sherril and I looked at each other in awe. It was just another confirmation that the Holy Spirit was with us. Reverend Mary listened as we shared the details of Daniel's condition, and the next day, she delivered a beautiful handmade quilt to his room.

Daniel's hospital room was filled with so many cherished gifts of faith. The day of his cardiac arrest, when I'd asked my friend Lisa to please bring a rosary with her, one of them that she brought to us was a special rosary that was given to her, and Lisa told us the story about how the beads of that particular rosary had been made from crushed rose petals. We knew that roses are considered to be the sign of the Blessed Mother, and we had also received a Mass card from a kind neighbor with St. Therese of Lisieux, known as "The Little Flower of Jesus." Roses are believed to be St. Therese's sign that God is listening and will respond. Jimmy and I hung Lisa's special rosary – made of crushed rose petals – on Daniel's bedpost.

Daniel had been given a small bottle of Holy Water from the Jordan River when he was baptized by our Deacon Lee. We often used the water to bless Daniel and even sprinkled it on his surgeons, doctors, and nurses before procedures. It may have appeared superstitious to some, but we loved that even Daniel's surgeon (who was Jewish) allowed me to sprinkle Holy Water on him and indicated that he was willing to accept any help in the name of our Lord.

Deacon Lee and his wife, Alice, frequently visited us in the hospital and became a true source of comfort to Jimmy and me. In fact, on the few occasions when we were too concerned to reach out to our families, we often called upon Deacon Lee for words of encouragement and faith. Jimmy and I were so blessed to have him (and his wife) there for us both physically and spiritually.

Another sister-in-Christ for me to lean on was my friend Carmen, Ami Mei's mom. She came to visit often and would always insist that we gather around Daniel's bed and join our hands in prayer while she was there. Whenever Jimmy and I requested specific prayers for our son, we knew that Carmen would literally hit her knees. She adored her "little buddy," Daniel.

Jimmy and I were also visited in the hospital by a dear friend named Dana who'd touched our family years before with her faith and grace when her six-year-old son, Stephen, had suffered from leukemia and it tragically took his life. It had literally been years since Dana and I had spoken, but the minute she heard about Daniel, Dana picked up the phone to call me and drove down to visit us that day. Dana knew precisely what my husband and I were going through emotionally. After all, she and her husband had spent *years* in the hospital caring for their son, Stephen, during his long battle with leukemia.

Dana brought an arsenal of Catholic and religious relics with her and prayed over Daniel's sick little body. She also used Reiki (Rei meaning "God's Wisdom or the Higher Power," and Ki meaning "life force energy"), which is a Japanese technique for stress reduction and relaxation administered by "laying hands" on the patient. It is based on the idea that an unseen "life force energy" flows through us and is what causes us to be alive. Neither Jimmy nor I had ever heard of this practice, and we were entirely unaware of its origins. All we knew was that a good Catholic sister-in-Christ – out of love – was trying to help our son. If you've never had a medically fragile child, all of this might be difficult to relate to, but we were willing to try anything to save Daniel's life, especially if it was of a spiritual nature.

Our neighbor and friend, Margaret, brought us something that her mother, Judy, had insisted that Jimmy and I receive. It was oil from the Weingarten Abbey monastery in Germany. Based on the small hand-written label from this unassuming glass bottle, I researched this Holy oil online, and was astonished to find information on the Internet about this relic, which – according to legend – has traces to the Holy Blood of Jesus. It is known as "The greatest treasure of Weingarten," and is still supposedly preserved in the church!

The history-book story claims that Longinus (the Roman soldier who opened Jesus' side with a lance) caught some of the Sacred Blood and preserved it in a lead box, which he later buried. It was miraculously discovered in 804 and solemnly exalted by Pope Leo III, but buried again during the Hungarian and Norman invasions. In 1048, it was re-discovered and solemnly exalted by Pope Leo IX in the presence of the Roman emperor Henry III, and many other dignitaries. It was divided into three parts, one of which was taken to Rome by the pope, one was given to the emperor, Henry III, and the third remained at Mantua.

Henry III bequeathed his share of the relic to Count Baldwin V of Flanders, who gave it to his daughter, Juditha. After her marriage to Guelph IV of Bavaria, Juditha presented the relic to the town of Weingarten. The solemn presentation took place in 1090, on the Friday after the feast of the Ascension, and it was stipulated that annually on the same day (which came to be known as Blutfreitag), the relic should be carried in solemn procession. The procession was prohibited in 1812, but since 1849, it has taken place every year and is popularly known as the *Blutritt*. The relic is carried by a rider (der heilige Blutritter) on horseback, followed by many other riders, and thousands of people on foot. The reliquary (formerly of solid gold and set with numerous jewels and valued at about 70,000 florins) was confiscated by the Government during the suppression of the monastery and replaced by a gilded copper imitation. We were amazed to find that this was the very oil I had been rubbing on our little boy's body.

Chapter Nineteen

UPS AND DOWNS

Each day at the hospital brought a whirlwind of new and unfamiliar medical jargon and terminology as part of a learning experience that Jimmy and I never expected to have. My husband and I constantly felt as if we were on a rollercoaster ride with extreme and intense ups and downs.

Since I can't bring myself to relive many of those moments in the hospital (and truly can't remember much of what I'd learned at the time), I've decided to rely largely on my blog postings to tell the story of those harrowing days.

TODAY IS A BIG DAY | May 17, 2010

Our focus of concern has switched to Daniel's kidneys this morning. We were prepared for this because they saw it coming. His BUN levels have elevated and urine output has significantly decreased. Daniel's doctors had planned to insert a catheter today in the probable event that dialysis will take place.

On a good (but anxious) note, they are going to try to remove Daniel from the ECMO machine today. We are prepared that this might not be successful right away, but of course we are praying for the best here. We are told his lung x-ray has improved again.

PLAN "B" | May 17, 2010

"In God We Trust." Happy moments, praise God. Difficult moments, seek God. Quiet moments, worship God. Painful moments, trust God. Every moment, thank God.

So, we've gone to plan B, since Daniel went into renal failure this morning. After rounds, the surgeon and the team have decided it is in Daniel's best interest to stay on ECMO while they deal with his kidneys. We are not looking at this as a 'setback' but rather as a 'set-aside'. They had warned us of this possibility, and leave it to Daniel (Murphy's Law) to give us a run for our money again! Little Bugger. In God we trust...

DIALYSIS | May 17, 2010

As I write, the doctors are ramping up for some surgical procedures on Daniel. After "negotiations" between the Nephrology team and the Surgical team, they have decided to utilize the ECMO machine for his kidney dialysis, since the lines are already set up. They have also decided to insert a catheter into his abdomen for the purpose of draining fluid and to use in the event of another dialysis option. They are also going to change some lines to his heart. Hang in there, buddy. Hang in there.

WEATHERING THE STORM | May 18, 2010

Philippians 4:6-7 — "Be anxious for nothing, but in every-thing, by prayer and supplication, with Thanksgiving let your requests be known to God. And the peace of God, which transcends all understanding, will guard your hearts and your minds in Christ Jesus."

Our Aunt Karen called with this Bible verse yesterday just at the time I was crawling out of my skin. Yesterday was a rollercoaster. We were across the street at dinner when my cell phone rang. It was the hospital saying that they needed permission to insert a larger catheter for Daniel's dialysis. Just hearing the Doctor's voice on the other end sent my stomach into knots.

We rushed back to the hospital. Thank the good Lord, the catheter was inserted just fine without any bleeding at all. We decided to stick around for a while since there seemed to be a lot of commotion around Daniel's room as they tried to stabilize the dialysis process. Apparently, the first three hours can be really rocky, especially with Daniel on the ECMO machine, too. At around 9:00 p.m., the surgeon calmly, but gravely, stated that Daniel's chest was bleeding and he was going to have to go in. Our hearts sank. Here we go again. It was a very long couple of hours as Jimmy and I watched, waited, and prayed. At anxious moments, we decided to pace the hallway and pray. At 11:00 p.m., we received the news that brought joyous tears and more thanks to God.

The bleeding had stopped, the dialysis was working, and Daniel was stable. We were able to rest last night knowing that everyone in there would watch him like a hawk. This morning the sky is bright blue. We walked into smiling faces and a stable little boy. His BUN and creatinine levels are drastically decreased. His heart is pacing better. The plan today is to continue dialysis, and they will possibly even wean him from ECMO some more.

PRAYING FOR MOVEMENT | May 18, 2010

At noon today, the doctors decided to give Daniel a "Roc Holiday." They removed him from his paralytic drug, Rocuronium. They do this to find out how long it takes the body to react. Once Daniel's body shows signs of movement, which can even be twitching, they will begin administering the drug once again. It is for his own safety right now, with the ECMO machine and the fact that his chest is still open. So this evening we pray for movement.

GOALS FOR THE DAY | May 19, 2010

First of all, thank you for so many inspirational emails and posts this morning. Thank you for keeping us focused and for sharing your love. We feel it. Daniel hasn't moved yet, but they are not alarmed given his sick kidneys. It may take a day or so for his body to clear the medication. Today's issues are a high white cell count and high lactic acid levels. They are sending cultures out to check for infection and they are doing some 'balancing' to adjust the acid levels. I will post again once we meet with the team this morning. I'd like to post some good news!

PRAYERS FOR A STRONG HEART & LUNGS! | May 19, 2010

We just got wind that they feel Daniel's heart and lungs are doing well enough to try to remove him from the ECMO machine today! They will keep him connected in the event his body isn't ready, but all signs are saying it is. Please, please pray for this little guy's body to stand strong.

URGENT PRAYER REQUEST | May 19, 2010

We just found out that though they are removing him from ECMO, it is out of necessity because other organs appear to be at risk right now. They are very concerned about his white cell count being up. We need prayers that he can survive without ECMO and that his body will handle things better. They are taking him off now. We pray he hangs tough.

TRYING AGAIN TOMORROW | May 19, 2010

Daniel held his own off the ECMO machine, but given his high white cell counts and a rise of lactic acid in his blood, they decided to return him to ECMO after about an hour. They will work on figuring out why these issues are occurring. They will try again tomorrow to remove him from the machine. His lungs are at the bottom of the priority list now. His kidneys are still being looked at, so they will return to dialysis. We stand strong for Daniel. We know you are praying hard. Oh, and I should mention that, thanks to a dear friend, Daniel has a beautiful statue of the Blessed Mother in his room looking down on him. We know this will bring him comfort and protection.

I remember that day, thinking to myself in a panic, that we needed a statue of the Blessed Mother in Daniel's room. That same morning, unbeknownst to us, our friend Tabitha was having a conversation about Daniel with her brother, Jeremiah, and they cried together as they recalled her brother's own medically critical past in his early twenties when he suffered a brain aneurysm that literally took him years to recover from. During Jeremiah's critical time – in the very same hospital where Daniel was being treated – someone had given him a statue of the Blessed Mother.

This statue was with Jeremiah during his recovery and his family believes that it helped pull him through and restore him to health. Jeremiah decided (while talking with Tabitha that morning) that Daniel needed to have his statue with him. As the Holy Spirit's timing would have it, this special statue was immediately delivered to Sherril, and she gave it to my parents so they could bring it to the hospital that day.

In retrospect, it is truly comforting to know that the Blessed Mother was shining down on Daniel as he took his last breaths. I could almost envision her holding Daniel in her arms.

And while we were comforted that Daniel was being watched over by our Blessed Mother, I was receiving Holy comfort of my own. Twice during our stay in the Ronald McDonald House, I encountered a spiritual phenomenon. Please bear with me as I attempt to explain it properly. I would often lie in bed praying myself to sleep while holding Daniel's teddy bear and my clutch cross. On two separate occasions, I was in bed and my eyes were closed, but I was not asleep – so I know I wasn't dreaming. A beam of white light entered my body and flooded my entire being. I was filled with a fleeting (but strong) sensation of peace and warmth that suddenly made me feel very safe and comfortable, and I remember feeling as if the Holy Spirit had just poured His strength into me to get me through this medical ordeal. It actually seemed that *as I was praying*, I was receiving the strengthening Grace of God to deal with Daniel's condition and what was to come.

Chapter Twenty

WALKING WITH GOD

It seemed that my posts (and probably my understandably exhausted state of mind) were becoming too pessimistic, and my own father had even decided to field his questions to Jimmy instead of me because he felt that I was too negative to talk to. I had decided not to share one incident that happened in the hospital on the blog because I just thought this particular setback would put our friends and followers over the edge.

I was trying with every fiber of my being to be optimistic about Daniel's situation, but something was blocking the light – like a dark cloud – and telling me otherwise. Daniel's test reports continued to indicate the presence of a systemic infection, but the nurses – who were constantly swabbing every chest tube site – still couldn't identify its source.

On Wednesday, May 19th, Daniel's right foot began to look noticeably mottled. Early in the day, I mentioned Daniel's strange-looking foot to his nurse. At that time, it hadn't really changed color much, but I did notice the beginning of its mottled appearance. Throughout the day, the nurse kept watch on Daniel's foot until his surgeon finally came by around 4:00 p.m. before he departed for the day.

The surgeon took one look at Daniel's foot and was confident that Daniel's dialysis catheter line was the source of the systemic infection. Evidently, the line had caused an arterial blockage in

Daniel's right leg that was causing poor profusion and lack of blood circulation to his right foot. Daniel's surgeon immediately called for the line to be re-routed to his left leg, yet another agonizing procedure for our son to endure. Before the surgeon left that day, we had a disturbing, but necessary, exchange. "I think we need to know what's *really* going on here," I said to him in exasperation.

The surgeon knew exactly where my statement was headed. He nodded his head and replied, "We will take a very serious evaluation if and when the time becomes necessary." I had called the surgeon out on Daniel's condition because I just wanted the truth – and he had taken the bait. Don't get me wrong – I wasn't giving up hope. I would have sat in that hospital every day for a year (or more) if it meant bringing Daniel home, but my motherly instinct did not want them to start doing needless procedures if our little boy's fate was to leave this earth. So far, it had just seemed to be one thing after another for poor Daniel, and we weren't keen on the idea of torturing our son.

Jimmy and his father peered angrily at the surgeon with disbelief, both feeling totally betrayed. They were raging inside and, quite frankly, I think the surgeon was lucky that he didn't get punched out by two irate Irishmen. This was the first time we'd heard something so bleak come from the surgeon, and the first indication that he thought (even remotely) there was a chance Daniel might not make it. I attempted to calm the guys down, and we moved out into the hallway where I could rationally explain my exchange with the surgeon to Jimmy and my father-in-law. Grandpa Murphy was overwhelmed and exhausted by the very idea of Daniel not surviving, and it was simply too much for him to bear, so we decided that he should drive home and try to get some sleep. Jimmy and I were not ready to leave the hospital just yet – not until we knew more about what was going on with our son.

At about seven o'clock that night, the pediatric surgery team came by to take a look at Daniel's foot, and they told us that his arterial blockage could very possibly turn into a more serious situation. In fact, they believed that our son's right foot might have to be amputated if the condition worsened. Just when we needed it, the Holy Spirit was woven into our evening to give us hope. A nurse named Joy, who could see the anguish in my eyes, walked directly to me holding a small black Bible. She looked into my eyes in a piercing way that I'll never forget, and in the calmest voice said, "Psalm 91. Read Psalm 91."

If you aren't familiar with it, Psalm 91 is often referred to as the "Psalm of Protection." I immediately began to intensely study the Bible she had handed me, concentrating on this Psalm over and over in an attempt to fully comprehend the words. But with all the anxiety I was feeling at the moment, it was hard for me to grasp the entirety of His message. There were two verses that I focused on – two and four. Verse Two stated, "I will say of the Lord, He is my refuge and my fortress: my God; in him will I trust." Verse Four stated, "He shall cover thee with his feathers, and under his wings shalt thou trust: his truth shall be thy shield and buckler." These verses provided comfort and renewed our hope. The full text of Psalm 91 (King James Version as given to me by Nurse Joy) can be found in the Appendix.

Jimmy and I went back to the Ronald McDonald House later that evening feeling very uncertain about Daniel's fate, and we were still very anxious despite our faith in God's mercy. We were awakened at 11:18 p.m. by a harrowing phone call when the doctors called us to say that they needed to do an emergency procedure on

Daniel's foot and leg. Jimmy's cell phone rang first, but as Murphy's Law would have it, his phone was broken, and he wasn't able to answer incoming calls. My husband and I watched the phone ring and ring for what seemed like an eternity, and we were unable to do a darn thing about it. Then, as our hearts seemed to pound out of our chests, we waited. It seemed like hours, yet it was merely seconds before my cell phone rang. I did not have the guts to answer my phone, so my husband bravely took charge and answered – only to hear that Daniel's right foot had become the "serious problem" that they'd hoped it wouldn't.

In a panic, Jimmy and I literally ran from the Ronald McDonald House through the long corridor over to the hospital to meet the surgeons. By that time, Daniel's foot and leg from the calf down were the alarming color of a dark purple eggplant. It was horrific to see how his foot's appearance had changed from earlier in the evening. The surgical team explained the emergency procedure to Jimmy and me, and pleaded that we really had nothing to lose by trying to loosen any blood clots that they could find. Their hope was to remove some clots and create profusion and blood flow to Daniel's foot again since it obviously was not receiving either. Jimmy and I were so emotionally distraught that we insisted they call Daniel's surgeon to come to the hospital. We were both confused and concerned, and we just wanted him there to assist. By the time the surgeon arrived, Jimmy and I had already signed the consent forms and given the surgical team our "go ahead."

Shortly thereafter, my husband and I were approached by one of the members of the pediatric surgical staff – a young girl who was named Gia. I don't remember if she was actually an intern or a staff member. Gia had introduced herself to us earlier that afternoon, but this time – when we made eye contact – she looked different. Gia seemed nervous and concerned, and I could tell that she wanted to approach and speak with Jimmy and me.

After seeing the condition of Daniel's foot deteriorate through the evening, she had gone back to the wing of the hospital where she cared for a block of patients. One of them was a man who suffered from pancreatic cancer. His wife, named Francine, was a very religious woman who had become quite close to Gia. Francine had noticed the concern in Gia's eyes that evening and asked her what was the matter. Gia told her about the little boy named Daniel on the 5th floor of the pediatric I.C.U. She told Francine about our son's foot, and Gia told Francine that she was very concerned about Daniel's condition. Francine took Gia by the hands, and while tucking a Miraculous Medal of Mary into her palm, insisted that Gia deliver the medal to us. Gia had been nervous about giving Jimmy and me the medal because she did not know whether or not we were religious, and she didn't want to offend us in any way. But even through her uncertainty, Gia believed it was a delivery that she needed to make.

When Gia handed me the medal and told us the story of Francine, it gave me such comfort. The medal had performed nothing short of miracles for Francine's husband, and it was their hope that it would help Daniel, as well. We looked into Gia's eyes and told her how grateful we were for her gift – for Francine's gift. I told her how wonderful it was, in this world where people are so reluctant to mix medicine with love and emotions, that Gia had taken such a huge leap of faith to deliver this blessing to us. She looked at me with a stunned expression and confided that the very same words had come out of Francine's mouth when she'd handed the medal to Gia. She claimed to have "cutis anserine," the medical term for goose bumps, and together we reveled in the power of the Holy Spirit.

That night left Gia – who had not been a religious person before – with an overwhelming desire to explore her faith.

In our joint quest for consolation, Jimmy and I both attempted to call a few of our closest friends and family members before Daniel's emergency surgery began. Interestingly though, no one was available to take our calls. Sherril, who usually kept her cell phone on her nightstand every night in case we needed her, had – on that particular night – made the decision to leave her phone downstairs. Something inside had told her everything was okay that night. We had also tried to reach Grandpa Murphy, but in his state of pure exhaustion, he slept right through the call.

At that moment, Jimmy and I both knew that God was calling us – only us – to take a walk with Him. Hand in hand and arm in arm, my husband and I paced the hallways of the hospital together in the middle of the night. The fluorescent lights beamed brightly, and it was eerily quiet on the entire floor. The only activity in the P.I.C.U. was taking place in room 25, our son's room.

Oddly, neither of us could conjure up a single tear. Our bodies and our minds were in fight mode – in prayer mode – and it seemed that God was preparing us for the possibility that we might lose Daniel. Together, we lamented about how we did not want to lose our son, but Jimmy and I agreed that we did not want him to suffer. Nor did we want extraordinary measures to take place if God wanted him. We then pleaded with God again that we still longed to be a family of four. Our thoughts bounced around like ping pong balls, and while our brains tried desperately to rationalize the "what ifs," we weren't at all prepared to lose Daniel.

Jimmy and I paced those hallways for several hours before the surgeon, who looked like he'd been through Hell wearing sweat-soaked scrubs, came out to deliver the welcome news that Daniel's foot had likely been saved and that the procedure had helped to successfully loosen some clots. We were thoroughly relieved to hear this news, yet back at the Ronald McDonald House, Jimmy and I went to bed knowing that Daniel clearly wasn't "out of the woods." That night – by speaking to us loudly and clearly in the hospital hallways – God had prepared us for the possibility of what was yet to come.

The next morning, Jimmy and I made phone calls to our family and close friends on our way over to the hospital. We were exhausted, terrified, and mentally preparing for the worst. We ran into Gia on the hospital elevator, and she was overjoyed with Daniel's condition – proclaiming that the talk of the hospital was "the miracle on the 5th floor." Yes, miraculously, Daniel's leg and foot were practically back to normal, except for only the tips of his toes, which were still very dark purple! The doctors explained that his toes had suffered the equivalent of serious frostbite and were gangrenous. It was likely that – though the condition of his foot would improve day by day – the feeling in his toes would probably never recover. Suddenly, our day wasn't looking so bleak – our son was not going to lose his right foot as we'd thought. In addition to our miracle, Daniel's surgeon had decided that the time had come to remove him from the ECMO machine. The events of that 24-hour period were a lot to digest in a short time, and a lesson to never underestimate the power of prayer.

ROMANS 12:12 | May 20, 2010

"Be Joyful in hope, patient in affliction, faithful in prayer."

Today we try again. We are still facing the same setbacks with Daniel's kidneys and liver and his white cell counts. God willing, he will stand strong on his own today. He is such a tough little guy.

My brother, Andrew, had heard the fear in our voices that morning and decided to immediately fly down from New Hampshire. It was so great to have him here with us. It was unfortunate that this would be Uncle Andrew's only time with Daniel, but we are so grateful that Daniel got to hear his voice, feel his touch, and know his love.

Aunt Diane and Uncle Rick decided to drive down from New Smyrna Beach to see Daniel that day, too. Aunt Diane is Grandma Pauline's cousin, and she and Uncle Rick are truly like an extra set of parents to us and grandparents to the kids. They absolutely adore Madi and they instantly adored Daniel, as well. We were thankful that they'd made it to our house to meet Daniel in the spring and spent time with us. On this day, I had asked them to drive down knowing that Jimmy and I really needed their support.

I had been calling Aunt Diane regularly for spiritual guidance because she had sort of become one of my pillars of faith. Before we traveled to China to bring Madi home, Aunt Diane and Uncle Rick had given us a beautiful clutch cross that I became glued to during Daniel's stay in the hospital. I brought it to the P.I.C.U. and held this clutch cross at practically every moment possible. I just couldn't physically put it down, and I even slept with it held tightly against my chest every night. That cross gave me so much comfort and constantly reminded me that God was with us every step of the way.

The last time I had spoken with Aunt Diane that morning, Daniel's condition had looked worrisome (from our perspective) based on the events of the night before. And the next time I spoke with them was when they had arrived at their hotel in Miami at around 5:00 p.m. When they called me, I failed to give them an explanation or an update of the day's events and just asked them to please hurry over to the hospital. Aunt Diane and Uncle Rick had no idea that Daniel's surgeon had – earlier in the day – decided to remove him from the ECMO machine, and they arrived just before the surgical team was removing the tubes. When they showed up at the front desk and asked for Daniel's room, they were told by the front desk, "The family is around the corner."

Unbeknownst to us, their hearts sank. When they made it around the corner to see us, both Aunt Diane and Uncle Rick had severely bloodshot eyes. It was evident that they had been crying quite a bit, and I remember feeling so perplexed about the way they looked, but I failed to question them because I was so caught up in the moment. They had thought (based on my exasperation that morning) that Daniel's removal from the ECMO machine meant he wasn't going to make it and that they were unplugging him from life support.

To their surprise, Aunt Diane and Uncle Rick were greeted by Daniel's cheerleading squad – all happy, hopeful faces, confident that our strong little boy would pull through. There were at least twelve of us there watching and waiting for Daniel to be free of the ECMO machine.

It was such a turnaround from the previous day! The energy in the P.I.C.U. was unexplainable. I believe even the doctors felt the intense positive energy amongst our group. Jimmy and I are still not sure if they expected Daniel to pull through as strongly as he did. He had – once again – defied the odds, showed remarkable strength, and exhibited an incredible will to live. We all left the hospital together and went to the patio bar that evening where we enjoyed a nice relaxing dinner and celebrated the wonderful day that had started out feeling so hopeless.

YAY, YAY, YAY DANIEL JAMES MURPHY | May 20, 2010

Daniel's totally on his own now with chest tubes removed and holding strong! His lung function is still supported by a ventilator, and they are pacing his heart until his body proves to be stable. We are told to expect a very bumpy 36 hours to come with blood pressure issues and other issues that they will continue to stay on top of.

Today brought many family visitors including my brother, Andrew, who flew in from NH today to be here for Daniel. Our Aunt Diane and Uncle Rick showed up, too (upon special request). Best friend Sherril has been here all day as Daniel's cheerleader – and ours too, along with other very dear friends. We fielded many loving phone calls and emails of inspiration and prayers.

May God bless all of you for the love and support you've given to Daniel and to our family. We'll never be able to acknowledge all of the special people who have so lovingly prayed for Daniel. So many of you we don't even know. We are so blessed. Daniel has obviously touched many lives.

Chapter Twenty-One

BABY STEPS

At this point, Daniel had been in the hospital for ten days, and Jimmy and I were physically, mentally, and emotionally spent. For this chapter, I have – once again – decided to rely on some of our blog posts, which so accurately depict our day-by-day trials with Daniel's condition. I want to mention how thankful I am to all of you who give blood. I cannot even imagine how much blood our son received through transfusions in the hospital, but it truly opened our eyes to the extreme need for blood supply, especially for people with rare blood types.

PRAISING THE LORD FOR A QUIET NIGHT | May 21, 2010

We had a feeling last night would be uneventful in a good way. Last night was an important night for Daniel to rest and us too! He was stable throughout the night! His night nurse also reported that he responded to the flashlight when she checked his eyes and he moved one of his feet, which indicates that the paralytic was finally processing out of his system. For his safety, they began to administer the drug again.

This morning he is having some blood pressure swings, but that is normal during this time, so they will tweak medications. We haven't been able to find out about his lab results yet but we should know more this morning, so I will post again. Thanks be to God!

SWITCHING GEARS PRAYER WARRIORS | May 21, 2010

The doctors feel like Daniel's body is getting stable enough to begin assessing his neurological condition. Though they began administering the paralytic again last night, Daniel's surgeon pulled him off it completely this morning. It will still take time to filter through his body but they want him to wake up to some degree. The poor little guy is puffed up like a marshmallow because they are giving him so much blood product in order to keep his blood pressure steady along with other fluids. He still isn't excreting urine, which isn't helping. We really need him to start peeing! The labs are looking good, thank God. His lactic acid is down. White counts are still a bit messed up because of his bone marrow being "revved up." His blood gases are normal. Day by day...

DANIEL IS SQUEEZING! | May 21, 2010

What unexplainable JOY we just experienced! Jimmy went in to see Daniel, and he squeezed Jimmy's finger!!! He called me in, and Daniel squeezed my finger, too!! What an overwhelming moment – obviously very emotional in an awesome way. They are going to let him come off a little more, and then they have to put Sleeping Beauty back to sleep for a while! Rejoice, rejoice. Thank you, God.

DANIEL WENT PEE PEE | May 21, 2010

I never thought I'd be so happy to announce this!!! Daniel produced about 10 cc's of urine!!! He's still squeezing away, too, and even starting to move his arms a little. I think this might be the best Friday we've ever had!!! Praise, praise, praise the Lord.

ANOTHER STABLE NIGHT | May 22, 2010

We are so thankful for "uneventful!" Daniel had a quiet night. He seems to save the action for early morning. Both mornings so far, he's had blood pressure issues, which they've managed to correct with medications. He didn't produce any urine last night, so they may put him back on dialysis. A few of his labs were a little off, too. He is still squeezing away this morning and moving his lips. They will not put him back on the paralytic now unless they absolutely need to. They will work with him through sedation.

We know there are still hills to climb, but we feel so strongly that he's turned a corner. We also feel strongly that we've turned another corner — in our faith. This experience has truly transformed us. I hope someday we can share some of the grace-filled moments we've been blessed with through this experience, with so many amazing people - unexplainable events that could only be driven by the Holy Spirit. Bubba, Grandpa, and Uncle Andrew are coming today to sit with Daniel while we drive back to Delray with Madi and spend the day with her. We are so looking forward to seeing her. It feels like it's been a month.

DANIEL IS OPENING HIS EYES | May 23, 2010

Upon return to the hospital yesterday, we received the amazing news from our family that Daniel was blinking while we were gone! He was also pretty active and moving around. He didn't move much for us at that time, and you could tell he was pretty deep in sleep. When we came back from dinner to say goodnight to Daniel, he totally responded to our voices! He opened his eyes and was squeezing our fingers tightly. Needless to say, we had a good night's sleep!

This morning brings much of the same. He is opening his eyes and moving. In fact, last night they had to give him more sedation because he was "too awake!" They stopped the main dialysis machine because the peritoneal dialysis seems to be picking up speed and adequately removing fluid. They have decreased the flow on his oscillating ventilator, which means his lungs are doing more of the work. They have a goal of Monday or Tuesday to close his chest. They want to make sure the swelling is down so nothing compromises his blood pressure.

Now is the time that Daniel needs more comforting than ever. We will be spending as much time in his room as we can just holding his hand, if nothing else. The power of prayer is awesome.

A NOTE ABOUT THE BABIES HERE | May 23, 2010

We noticed from the beginning how many babies are here in P.I.C.U. with no one visiting them. Through this absolute angel we met in the room next to Daniel's, we found out that some of these babies have been basically abandoned in the P.I.C.U. Can you imagine?

This very special woman, named Monica, has adopted babies twice from this hospital floor. She'd lost a baby girl two years ago to a failed organ transplant and then decided to adopt a very special little boy from the floor. He will be five next month. When Monica and her husband adopted him at two years of age, five of his failing organs had already been transplanted. He is now deaf from medications, and they just found out that he has cancer, so they've begun chemotherapy. His parents are here every day, selflessly giving their love to their little boy and always doing so with smiles on their faces.

Since we have the attention of so many dedicated prayer warriors, we ask that you please say some prayers for Logan, for his parents, and for all of the babies and children who are here "on their own."

MONDAY MORNING | May 24, 2010

No news is good news! Daniel is beginning to look more like Daniel. His swelling seems to be going down a bit. We are waiting for the doctors to do their rounds so we know the plan of action for the day. The night nurse said he was waking up more last night. Once I know more about the day, I promise I'll post again!!

SIDE STEPS TODAY | May 24, 2010

Today is about side steps. Daniel's swelling is going down, and he has put out a little urine today, thank God. The doctors have decided not to close his chest until they work on a couple of things. Daniel's diastolic pressure is up and they need to figure out why. They can't control this with medication without jeopardizing his kidneys, which they are not willing to do right now. They are also concerned about his platelet levels being low. They are going to do an echocardiogram today to take a closer look at his heart function and will aim for closing him tomorrow IF everything checks out okay. Thank you for helping us to remain strong. We pray that God will continue working miracles in Daniel's little body.

MAKING HEADWAY | May 25, 2010

It was another quiet night for Daniel. They were able to reduce his epinephrine levels a small amount. He lost more fluid, so his swelling continues to improve, albeit slowly. His chest x-ray showed some congestion, so they are going to break his ventilator circuit more often to suction out his chest. There are likely old clots and secretions that need to be cleared out. They have decided to wait another day on switching the ventilator. Chest closure may take place by week's end. We forgot to wish everyone Happy Pentecost on Sunday! We welcome the Pentecost season, which is all about the Holy Spirit and New Life!

Chapter Twenty-Two

OUR EMOTIONAL ROLLERCOASTER

The definition of *hope* is "the feeling that what is wanted can be had or that events will turn out for the best." My husband and I never lost hope. Even during the most difficult bumps in the road – that powerful four-letter word sustained us and gave us the fuel we needed to fight for our son.

A HOPEFUL DEVELOPMENT | May 25, 2010

Last Thursday, my dear friend Carrie called me to say that her Grandmother had called her that morning. Her Grandmother had this very strong feeling about Daniel. The message to us was, "Tell them to check the medication." Of course, our friend felt obligated to relay this information and I, of course, felt obliged to mention this to Daniel's doctors. On Saturday, the doctors began looking at making some changes and trying to find a reason why Daniel's platelet counts were so low despite the fact that they were giving him platelets. They began to suspect that Daniel might have sensitivity to Heparin, which was used throughout his time on the ECMO machine and was also used for his kidney dialysis.

Yesterday, the results came back that Daniel was "positive" for a reaction to Heparin. While Heparin usually acts as a blood thinner, in Daniel's system his antibodies began fighting the Heparin and it began clotting. He developed something called "HIT." (Andrew, look it up for me please!) We are hoping that this discovery will only lead to quicker healing. He still has some battles to overcome, but one can hope! Thank you God for sending your Holy Spirit to us and to the people in our lives during this time of need.

THANK GOD FOR QUIET NIGHTS! | May 26, 2010

We are always happy to report another one. They have been able to come down on his heart meds a bit, so Daniel is getting closer to chest closure. They want to strategize about the best way to get some more fluid off him first though. He produced 500 ml of urine in the past 24 hours, which was up from the day before. He is starting to look less puffy, too.

We feel good today. We feel positive. Thank God that Jimmy has been so strong through this while Mommy has had more than a few weak moments this week. I think I'm back on track now! Going to daily Mass at the Chapel here has really helped. The Lord's House has a way of comforting us and keeping us centered.

HIS CHEST IS CLOSED | May 26, 2010

It feels so strange not to have to "suit up" in a gown, gloves and mask! Daniel's chest has successfully been closed. I must admit that I became so used to suiting up, my inner germ-phobia makes me want to continue! My friend Carmen and I scurried off to 11:45 Mass while Jimmy waited with Bubba and Grandpa for the surgery to finish. We came back to a happy report that all went well. They will monitor him closely, especially in the area of blood pressures. In a few days, hopefully his lungs will have cleared enough for him to be switched from the oscillating ventilator (short bursts of air) to a traditional ventilator (longer bursts of air). Right now, we pray for healing of all organs so his body can move towards the next steps. Thank you for standing by our man.

AN ACTIVE NIGHT | May 27, 2010

Our little bugger gave 'em a run last night. In checking Daniel's diaper, the nurse found some odd sediment and discharge. It could be just "junk" from his poorly performing kidneys, but they are looking into it further. They have stopped his feeds for now, since he hasn't produced stool. His bowels could be "sleepy" from the paralysis meds he's been on periodically. He has a fever right now, which they are working on bringing down. Not surprising with everything his body went through yesterday.

Our highlights for the night were the fact that Daniel's heart is holding strong, and they were able to clear a good amount of secretion from his lungs! He is still producing a good amount of urine, though the quality of the urine isn't where it needs to be yet. We keep hearing that things should progress now that his chest is closed. We are praying that is true.

Today, we are going to surprise Madi and show up for her "end of year" school performance and take her out to lunch. We are so excited to see her smiling face. Friends Lisa and Sherril will be here today to sit with Daniel, so we can relax and enjoy our time with Madi. Lisa and Sherril are both bringing lots of books to read to Daniel!

BACK IN MIAMI | May 27, 2010

First, I must say that we had a great time seeing Madi today as she sang with her classmates on stage. She performed so well. The look on her face was of pure shock when she saw us in the audience. She was totally surprised. It seemed as if she was looking for Daniel's face in the crowd, too. Once the reality hit that we were actually there, she couldn't stop smiling!

We went to lunch together and spent some time playing chess (Bubba's been teaching her) before it was time to head back. She was sad when we left, but apparently that went away once we turned the corner! We received Madi's first report card – straight A's!!! She's such a great student. We will miss Mrs. Bivins, and feel so fortunate to have had her as Madi's first teacher.

As I write, Daniel's blood is being washed through a dialysis-like process called plasma exchange. This is supposed to help his kidneys start working effectively again by cleansing some of the junk out of his blood. This process will take a couple of hours. He's had a high fever all day, but I've watched it drop point-by-point since we returned at 4:00 p.m. The plasma exchange should help with the fever, too. It seems they are determined not to leave anything on the table when it comes to treating Daniel...

When Jimmy and I returned to the hospital to find out about the plasma exchange that I posted about, it caught us both by surprise, and we were seriously concerned. It felt like the events of that day gave us another forewarning from above. It just seemed as if they were taking such extreme measures – and they were. They really were trying everything possible to get Daniel's poorly performing organs to work again.

I remember being at our son's bedside – in tears – when they started the process. It felt so foreign, though they continued to reassure us that this was a good thing. In my utmost moment of despair, Amanda the anesthesiologist appeared out of nowhere, like an angel, and handed me a beautiful rosary. With her reassuring smile, she offered me a hug and said, "I noticed that Daniel only had two rosaries on his bedposts, and I thought he needed another one." She was such an angel to Jimmy and me – always showing up at the exact time when we needed a hug or reassurance. And she seemed to always be there to remind us that this would be a slow and lengthy process and that we needed to remain patient.

That evening, something else happened that my husband had not revealed to me until after Daniel had passed away. That night of the plasma exchange, Jimmy had a dream that he kept to himself for fear of upsetting me, which is very typical of my hyper-protective husband. The dream was very vivid and real to him – the kind that wakes you up out of a dead sleep with that eerie feeling that sends shivers down your spine. He and Daniel were swimming in the ocean. It was very, very dark, but Jimmy could see lights on the shore. They were both bobbing in the water together. Jimmy could not see our son's face – only the outline of his head. As Daniel began to struggle to stay afloat, Jimmy tried to reach for him, but they couldn't connect.

Daniel said, "Daddy, I can't do it anymore. I can't keep my head above the water," and he peacefully surrendered to the forces that pulled at him and disappeared into the water. As quickly as the dream began, it ended. Jimmy woke up in a cold sweat and never told me about it until after Daniel's death. His dream fascinated me. Was it merely an indication of Jimmy's uncertainty on a subconscious level? Or was it more…

"BEAUTIFUL" | May 28, 2010

Praise the Lord for those sweet words coming out of our night nurse's mouth! Daniel had a "beautiful night." The plasma exchange seems to be working. He is outputting a lot of urine since the treatment, and hopefully, its quality will be improved. Onward to lung function. The secretions in his chest are lessening.

The next goal will be to get Daniel off the oscillating ventilator. They had increased his support in the last few days with the big changes like closing his chest. Now that he's more stable, they will begin slowly weaning him again to make sure his lungs can handle it. We are also told that time is needed for Daniel's blood pressures to stabilize. We have all the time in the world to wait for our precious boy's body to heal.

That day, Jimmy and I had an epiphany. We had been so preoccupied, and it occurred to us that since not seeing Daniel was really bothering Madi, it would probably be therapeutic for Daniel to hear Madi's voice, too – I mean more of *her* voice, not the tape recording in his stuffed bear. We might have come up with the idea sooner if we'd thought it would be acceptable in the P.I.C.U. Luckily, the nurses had no objection, so "Madi Therapy" began. We called Madi on speakerphone to talk to Daniel.

Even though he couldn't respond verbally, he did wiggle, blink, and even tried to smile when he heard Madi's voice! It was simply magical, and it brought tears of joy to our eyes to see him respond so favorably. Daniel knew exactly whose voice that was, and Jimmy and I believed that this would be an imperative part of his healing process. We knew that being able to communicate with Daniel helped Madi too, so we decided to make a daily routine out of it.

♡

Chapter Twenty-Three

SLIPPING AWAY

On the heels of positive progress with Daniel's baby steps of healing, Jimmy and I felt it would be a good time to give our daughter
a surprise visit back at home. Though the idea of being far from
Daniel for the evening was uncomfortable, we knew it would be a
healthy departure for the two of us, both physically and emotionally.

At the beginning of the last chapter, I wrote about the definition
of hope, and how Jimmy and I never lost that feeling, that longing
for Daniel's life story to turn out for the best. But who – ultimately –
defines what "for the best" means? That's when faith storms in.

SATURDAY MORNING | May 29, 2010

The Holy Spirit sent us a spontaneous message to drive
home to Delray yesterday at around 4:00 p.m. Daniel had
a stable day, and we really wanted to see Madi. We feel like
she's beginning to need us more and more even though she's
doing so well with Bubba and Grandpa keeping her busy.
We had a pizza party, and I slept with Madi in her bed. We
tried to do a sleepover in our room, but she loves her bed so
much that she decided we should move. It was great to see
her and cuddle with her again.

We drove back to Miami this morning. We knew it must have
been a quiet night, because our phones did not ring, but I

still always find myself holding my breath when we come back. Those are good moments for burying my thoughts in prayer to relax my anxiety.

Today, Daniel's temperature is actually very low and they are warming him. I think he is happy that we are back. He is still moving quite a bit and looking around. He is still on dialysis. We are waiting for the doctors to make their mid-morning rounds so we can find out what's happening in detail, but his nurse says that he had a quiet night. Daniel's Aunt Kathy (Jimmy's sister) is flying in this morning! It will be so comforting to see her. There is nothing better than being surrounded by family, friends, and the love of God.

I had a different, troubled feeling when we returned to the hospital that morning. Though Daniel had a quiet night, something within me was unsettled. His temperature fluctuation was bothersome, and throughout the course of the day, I found it difficult to leave him. I just felt the need to stay by his side constantly and caress his little hands and feet. I sang his favorite songs and read stories to him all morning. My sister-in-law, Kathy, arrived around lunchtime, and we met her downstairs in the hospital lobby. Grandpa Murphy decided to head home and gave us "kids" time to catch up. We went over to the patio bar, our usual, and decompressed over lunch. Jimmy and I wanted to prepare Kathy for what she would see and bring her up to date about Daniel's condition. I had my clutch cross with me, and I refused to set it down — even through lunch, which I barely ate. Then the three of us went back upstairs, and we all spent some time in the room with Daniel. He totally responded to Aunt Kathy and squeezed her hand like crazy. This was the first time they had met in person, though Daniel knew her voice from the phone and from Skype.

At that time, I noticed that Daniel's belly looked different – nothing alarming – but it did look tighter and more swollen to me than it had previously. They had taken x-rays of his stomach just days before and found nothing but "subcutaneous air," or that's what it appeared to be on the x-ray, anyway. Sheila and David (Daniel's Godparents) showed up with Murphy and Myles to visit Daniel and to see Kathy. Daniel was looking noticeably less swollen now in his face, so much so that they noted a difference, as well. I was glad to hear that, since being there every day (and seeing him constantly) clouded our son's progress in my eyes. I was much more uptight than usual that day.

"Does Lisa always act this way?" Kathy asked Sheila.

Sheila replied, "No, she definitely seems more nervous than usual."

I knew my emotions and behaviors had changed, as well. I found myself calling for the nurses and asking more questions than ever before. It seemed like the monitors were more inconsistent than they had usually been, and the beeping was nearly constant; I could barely stand it. The nurses couldn't seem to balance out Daniel's pressures, and I was starting to get really rattled about it. The nurses contended that it was possibly an issue with the sensors rather than Daniel's body causing the commotion.

For the first time during our hospital ordeal, I felt like Shirley MacLaine in the movie *Terms of Endearment* when she totally lost her cool and flipped out at the nurses' station. I desperately wanted to scream at them – at someone – but deep inside I knew they were doing everything they could.

After the rest of the family had left the hospital, Kathy and Jimmy decided to get out for a while, too. Once again, I found myself glued to Daniel. I just couldn't bring myself to leave his bedside most of that day. I massaged his arms and legs and softly sang to him. As I hummed "You are my Sunshine" into his soft little ears, I couldn't suppress the tears from falling. That was Grandma Pauline's favorite song, and I prayed that – at that moment – she was right there in the room with us.

When Jimmy and Kathy returned, we stayed with Daniel until – at approximately 6:00 p.m. – we were all hungry and decided that we needed a break from reality. The three of us elected to head out for a quiet dinner together, and we agreed that it would be best to leave the hospital grounds. So, we chose to go back to the water-front restaurant, Casablanca, where we had dined together with Daniel on the night before his surgery.

Prior to leaving the hospital, I inquired at length about the night staff that would be coming in at 7:00 p.m. We wouldn't be there for shift change, which bothered me since this was something we had become so accustomed to for peace of mind. That night, it was a totally different staff than we were used to, which left me feeling very insecure. Detecting my frenzied mental state, the nurses assured us that Daniel would be in good hands.

"Does Lisa always cry when she leaves Daniel?" Kathy asked Jimmy. I don't remember weeping as we left Room 25 that night, but that wasn't something I usually did when I left our son. I didn't realize it at the time, but I could feel him slipping away. The three of us did go out to dinner, though heavily weighing in the back of my mind was concern for our little boy who so desperately needed help.

For a change of scenery from the Ronald McDonald House, Jimmy and I chose to stay in Kathy's room at the nearby Marriott that night. At 1:18 a.m. (I distinctly remember the time), Jimmy's cell phone rang. As we scrambled to wake up and grab the phone, we *already knew* who was calling us. It was the call that Jimmy and I did not want to answer, but we knew we had to. The attending physician on the other end of the call told Jimmy that we should come to the hospital immediately. At that moment, we both had this sinking feeling that we were losing Daniel. I knew in my heart that this was it, and that our time with our son was limited.

Luckily for us, the hotel was in close proximity, yet it seemed like an eternity to drive to the hospital. There were unexpected road-blocks, and we couldn't get to Daniel quickly enough. My body began to tremble, and my teeth chattered uncontrollably as loud as castanets. My nerves had literally tied themselves in knots. Kathy stayed back at the hotel to wait for Grandpa Murphy to drive down from Boca Raton to pick her up. This was all obviously way too much for her to absorb in just one day.

We parked in the garage and quickly made our way over to the hospital. As we looked up at the 5th floor, we could feel nothing but dread wondering what was happening up there. I always made Jimmy walk into the P.I.C.U. first because I was afraid of what I would see. I was – quite honestly – frightened of what I would face as I turned that corner to Daniel's room. On that night, we turned that corner to see crying faces – our worst fear.

The bright, overhead lights were on in Daniel's room, and there was quite a stir going on. We quickly realized that they were admin-istering CPR, and Daniel's surgeon was present in the room trying to resuscitate him. The attending physician who had called us, and who had been in charge that night, came out to tell us they had been giving Daniel CPR for a while. As she spoke, I could see her lips moving, but somehow I couldn't comprehend what she was saying. *What on earth was this woman telling us?* She was explaining exactly what Jimmy and I didn't want to hear – how Daniel's stom-ach had become a *serious* problem.

We watched the events taking place inside Daniel's room without wanting to watch – sort of like the feeling you get when passing by a fatal traffic accident, only this was *our son* – our precious baby boy we had fallen in love with only months before. Jimmy and I were afraid to look, and we were afraid not to look. My heart raced as the world began to collapse around us, and I knew inside that we had to immediately begin praying for the Lord to take Daniel and end our son's suffering. I clutched my cross harder than I knew how to, and I began begging – loudly and clearly – *begging* God to please take him. I repeated those words over and over, chanting, "Please God, take him. Please God, take him. Please God, take him." In my heart I knew that Daniel had been through enough, and as painful as the prayer could be, it was time for his suffering to end.

We feared that single moment of truth – *losing him* – and then it happened. As Daniel's surgeon approached us, we felt the walls caving in around us. He stared sorrowfully into our eyes and said, "I think we should stop administering CPR now."

Acknowledging Daniel's suffering and trusting in the Lord, we wholeheartedly agreed, as painful as it was. *How could we not?* This was not about us. This was about Daniel, and we just wanted him to be safe in the arms of our Lord. In our hearts, we knew we would find a way to live through it. And then, just moments later, our baby boy was gone. Our dreams of his future – and of our family's future together – had just been shattered into a million tiny pieces.

It seemed like everyone on that floor had tears in their eyes. The odd thing was that neither Jimmy nor I really knew any of them. It was an entirely different staff than we were used to and had bonded with. It felt so surreal, yet we could see how deeply Daniel had impacted those people, too. They needed time to prepare Daniel's lifeless body so that we could go in to see him. They did not want us to see him in the condition he was in, so they cleaned up the blood from his body, removed all of the tubes from his body and wheeled all of the machines from his room. The nurses had put a large chair in the room so Jimmy and I could hold Daniel for a while. I watched my sweet Jimmy sob like a baby as he held his precious son in his arms for the last time. It broke my heart to see such devastation in my husband, who appears as such a brawny and strong man but is as sensitive as they come.

Jimmy and I requested a Catholic priest, but the chaplain on call was non-denominational. At that point, it really didn't matter to us – we just needed someone there who could lead us in prayer and comfort us. The chaplain stayed with us for a while and provided some beautiful and insightful words about Heaven and the end of Daniel's suffering in his broken little body.

My husband and I had seen several families lose their children in that hospital while we were there. We had watched them grieve, and we had mourned for them as they tried to figure out how to pick up the pieces of their lives and survive after such tragedy. We had witnessed their pain, unable to do anything but hug them and offer our sympathies. But even though Jimmy and I had received signs from the Holy Spirit in the hospital, the mere idea of that happening to our family had been subconsciously shelved *way* out of reach since the day Daniel was placed in our hearts.

Jimmy and I couldn't bring ourselves to call anyone. We knew that it would only worry our family, and there was nothing we could do at 3:00 in the morning. We sat with our baby, stroking his hair, and I sang to him for the last time. We caressed him and kissed that sweet face knowing we would never get another opportunity to feel his skin ever again. We held those sweet little hands and feet in full knowledge that we would never get to see them grow.

Oh Lord, how could this happen to him? How could you take him from us after everything it took to get him here?

A nurse entered our room and Jimmy and I were then faced with a barrage of overwhelming decisions to think about. "Do you want to donate his organs to science?" she asked. "Do you want an autopsy performed?"

We just weren't mentally prepared to think about such questions while we were in the middle of digesting the loss of our child. In our hearts, we felt that Daniel's body had been through so much already, and it seemed as if every organ in his body had failed him in the past nineteen days. The decisions were just too burdensome to think about in the middle of the night without any guidance, so we declined all of them. In hindsight, I wish we'd made the decision to donate his organs, provided any of them were still viable.

When Grandpa and Kathy arrived, we all hugged and cried together. I felt truly sad for Grandpa, who had become so tightly bonded with Daniel – especially having traveled with us to China to bring him home. We lamented about our journey to get Daniel and now our grief-filled journey's end. It all seemed so bitterly cruel to lose him, but we managed to – at least – chuckle at the thought that Grandma had won this battle and taken Daniel from us to be with her. After all, she needed a baby up there in Heaven to take care of, too. That thought gave us a sliver of joy and comic relief in an otherwise very dark moment. As Sherril later quipped, "Grandma Pauline probably knocked over Jesus to get to Daniel!"

The nursing staff presented us with a beautiful keepsake box filled with a mold they'd made us of Daniel's little hand and an assortment of grieving pamphlets. I asked if I could clip some of our son's hair to keep, too, and they kindly included that in the box for Jimmy and me. With broken hearts, we collected our belongings – Daniel's belongings

– blankets and rosaries, the statue of the Blessed Mother, "Glowy" and "Lucky" Bear, and everything else we owned in the room.

One of the blankets, a beautiful hand-crocheted blanket made for us by a parishioner at Madi's preschool, was stained with Daniel's blood. To this day, I still can't bear to wash that blanket, knowing that his blood is on it and that we still have a physical part of him; I know that sounds strange, but it's true. Sadly, along the way we lost two of the rosaries and one very special bear. We still – after all this time – haven't been able to find these items; we like to think that Daniel may have taken them with him.

We said our final goodbyes to our son, knowing that we had to leave the hospital at some point without the one thing that mattered to us the most – Daniel. It was very difficult to leave his body there, but we knew that *he* wasn't really there. His soul had already departed, and his body was finished doing its job. That made it slightly easier to bear knowing where he was, and we imagined that he must've been surrounded by angels and had wings of his own.

♡

Chapter Twenty-Four

TRINITY SUNDAY

The four of us walked over to the Ronald McDonald House in total silence, and then we cleared out our room. Grandpa and Kathy helped us pack up everything, and we sobbed intermittently as we packed up our belongings.

As I laid eyes on those items that I had taken for granted – Daniel's little shoes, his little clothes – it was far too much to deal with. We began to realize how sacred and precious those possessions would become to us now. Jimmy and I just wanted (and needed) to go home. It felt so strange to take off in the middle of the night like runaways, but we couldn't wait to leave Miami, as if the bad dream (that was our new reality) would be over when we did.

It was about 5:00 a.m. and I-95 was a freak show. Apparently, it was some special weekend in Miami, and the craziest drivers were still on the road. We opted – when given the chance – to jump on the less-congested turnpike, and we headed north towards Delray. We called Bubba and Grandpa at around 5:30 a.m. to break the news to them. How awful it was to report the news that their adored little grandson *was gone*. I knew that they were shocked and devastated, but both remained strong as fortresses and said that they would have some coffee ready for us. I remember walking to our front door where Bubba and Grandpa greeted and hugged both of us tightly, but without tears. My parents were so stoic – so strong. They let Jimmy and me do all the work. I knew they would have their moments, but right now they just wanted to be strong, supportive, and loving parents for the sake of their kids.

As we all sat in the living room anxiously waiting for Madi to wake up, that dreaded moment was eerily familiar to when Grandma Pauline had passed away just one year before. How do you tell a four-year old child that her little brother *isn't coming home*? Through the monitor, at around 6:30 a.m., we finally heard Madi stirring. Jimmy and I each took a deep breath and walked into her room, accompanied by "Glowy" (Daniel's musical seahorse) and his favorite blanket.

With tear-filled eyes, we broke the devastating news to Madi. We wept – she wept. She was so angry that she didn't get the chance to see Daniel again before he died, and she clearly – painfully – understood what had happened, and realized that she wouldn't get to see her little brother ever again. We carried her out into the living room to be with the rest of the family. Jimmy and I tried to answer her questions as they were asked of us, and we wept off and on as the waves of grief came crashing in.

It was so surreal that just the day before – yet it seemed so long ago – we had started calling Madi on speakerphone to talk to Daniel. And even though he couldn't respond to her verbally, he wiggled, blinked and even tried to smile when he heard her voice. It was simply magical, and at the time we believed that was a crucial part of his healing process. Now, it simply gave us comfort to know that Daniel had heard Madi's voice one last time before he left this earth. It was equally important that Madi knew her little brother had received her encouraging words and had clearly loved hearing her voice.

One by one, we made calls to break the news to our inner circle. It was as if no one on the other end of that phone could comprehend what we were saying to them. In retrospect, my blog entries up until that point had seemed so hopeful that no one expected this sad, sudden ending. Daniel's condition had turned so quickly from stable to unstable, and I think at that point, Jimmy and I still didn't even fully comprehend what had gone wrong with his body. All we knew for sure was that our precious son was gone.

At approximately 8:30 a.m., knowing that so many people were anxiously awaiting an update, I mustered up the strength to type this post on the blog:

OUR LITTLE ANGEL IN HEAVEN | May 30, 2010

Our dear Daniel went to Heaven in the middle of the night. He put up such a good fight, but his little body just couldn't take it anymore. The Good Lord needed another angel. We are sad, but we are so thankful. We are so thankful for every minute we had with Daniel, and wouldn't give one minute of it back. He was (is) such a beautiful little soul, and our lives are immeasurably richer for having had him in it.

God DID have a plan when he sent us halfway across the world to bring Daniel home. It just wasn't the plan we expected. We are so thankful that he experienced the love of our family and friends. We are so thankful that he was baptized at St. Vincent Ferrer. Though his time with us was short, he touched us deeply and managed to touch many, many people along the way. We can't thank everyone enough for the prayers, the love, and the support. We prayed him right home to Jesus. Daniel is in the best of hands now.

We are still in awe that Daniel went to Heaven on Holy Trinity Sunday, a celebration of the Father, Son, and Holy Spirit. It was such a gift, given the Holy Spirit's involvement during our entire journey, and it seemed like a clear message that everything was okay. During our time at the hospital, the Holy Spirit had given us so many subtle clues that Daniel was slipping away, but God always provided very non-subtle messages that Jesus was beside us every step of the way and that He felt our pain and now shared our grief. We have no doubt that He wept with us.

I remember that our friend Emily called me that morning with an unmistakable lump of sadness in her throat. As her voice quivered, Emily said to me, "Everything looks different today. The sky looks bluer. The clouds look whiter." Emily declared that the grass and trees were greener than she had ever seen them. And they were. We, too, had noticed that the day was absolutely perfect. It was as if the world was in high-definition, and Daniel's soul added to the atmosphere made everything more noticeably vibrant.

May 30th was a long morning, and a day with no sleep. How could we possibly sleep knowing that Daniel would still be gone when we woke up? While we embraced the loving support of our family, friends began to show up at the house to offer their sympathies and provide comfort in the best ways that they knew how – some with food, some with hugs, and others who chose to leave something at our doorstep. Each gracious act of kindness lifted our spirits and kept us from falling apart.

One of my closest friends, Carrie, and her family had been so helpful while we were in the hospital. Her family had taken Madi in on several occasions so Bubba and Grandpa could come to the hospital for a visit. Carrie was also a true sister in Christ to whom I could pour out my deepest fears and concerns when I needed to.

On the day that Daniel died, Carrie, (who happens to be a blogger, too) wrote the most beautiful post on her blog about faith:

Carrie's blog post

Phone rings early for a Sunday, Doug passes it to me when he sees the name on the Caller ID. Holding the phone, lying between girls, I hear her voice and for a minute I wonder if I am still dreaming. I sit up.

I hear, "He passed. Daniel is gone."

I ask foolishly "what happened?" as if it matters.

I already know. I have been following his story morning, noon, and evening along with so many others – hopefully, prayerfully holding this family up. After making pancakes, I check her blog, already a post of his passing, and I am struck by the choice she already made.

God does give us a choice. It is so maddening, but he gives that responsibility of choice to us.

The suffering is sure. Rain comes and saturates our world. We can choose to let the rain flood and overtake our hearts, make us choke on fear and helplessness, or we can choose to see it another way. See the way rain makes colors shimmer more vibrantly. Look beyond obvious beauty, look beyond and see it saturate the earth for bringing forth new buds of life. We can choose to wait expectedly hopeful for the rainbow.

True, there are days when seeing the colors seems impossible, and we may not want to strain to think of the hopefulness of new life or even believe in the promise of the rainbow. But it is always our choice, our *response-ability*.

When I visit, she even tells me, "Today is Holy Trinity Sunday, and it is such a beautiful day." She chooses to see. And by doing so, I feel empowered to choose to see, too. I can't help but appreciate the moment before me when I see how precious a moment can be. Because she allowed so many to be part of his [Daniel's] moments; his journey from halfway around the world to them, and then through his suffering. Her sharing of what she saw made so many feel the blessing of him, too.

They thank everyone for their prayers, for their hope, for sharing their spirit. She even acknowledges that this was God's plan all along. And though it is still very much a loss to them, they are still so grateful for what they were given. His life forever changed theirs. I want it to change mine too, I want to see and live with these eyes. These eyes brimming with tears will also brim full with deep joy because the suffering transforms hearts. Before Christ could rise, bone and flesh had to be pierced. When your world is tear washed, it cleanses your heart and enables the eyes to really see the beautiful, fleeting, and vibrant blessings to embrace them as such.

Chapter Twenty-Five

BLESSINGS

$\mathcal{W}e$ received so many comforting blessings from friends, family, and from the Holy Spirit on that day as well as that entire week.

Our friend, Clare, and her daughter, Emily, drove from Tampa to South Florida the minute they heard the news. Clare knew that Emily, who is Madi's soul mate (another little adopted China doll), would be the perfect distraction for her loss. Clare also knew that she would be able to help us that week as we plodded through the blur of grief. Both Clare and Emily were amazing. In fact, all of our friends were overwhelmingly supportive.

Over the next few days, friends and family members came by the house to give condolences and share their love. Monsignor Tom, from St. Vincent Ferrer, unexpectedly came by our house to offer prayers and bless our family and home. We were truly covered by a blanket of love and support from our entire community.

One of the most meaningful gifts we received was a copy of a poem written by Edgar Guest called "A Child of Mine" (also known as "To All Parents"). It brought us peaceful comfort, written with such a beautiful perspective.

A Child of Mine

"I'll lend you for a little time
A child of Mine." He said.
"For you to love the while he lives
And mourn for when he's dead.

It may be six or seven year
Or twenty-two or three
But will you, till I call him back
Take care of him for Me?

He'll bring his charms to gladden you
And should his stay be brief,
You'll have his lovely memories
As solace for your grief.

I cannot promise he will stay
Since all from Earth return,
But there are lessons taught down there
I want the child to learn.

I've looked this wide world over
In my search for teacher's true,
And from the throngs that crowd life's lanes,
I have selected you;

Now will you give him all your love,
Nor think the labour vain
Nor hate Me when I come to call
And take him back again?"

I fancied that I heard them say,
"Dear Lord, They will be done,
For all the joy Thy child shall bring,
For the risk of grief we'll run.

We'll shelter him with tenderness,
We'll love him while we may,
And for the happiness we've known,
Forever grateful stay.

But should the angels call for him
Much sooner than we planned,
We'll brave the bitter grief that comes
And try to understand."

Coordinating the details for Daniel's funeral was excruciating. Accompanied by Grandpa Murphy and Kathy, we went to the funeral home on Monday. Jimmy and I choked back tears as we sorted through books displaying pictures of urn after urn – little ones, big ones. Is there a more difficult task than choosing an urn for the remains of your two-year old son? I'm sure there must be, but at the time it certainly didn't seem so to us. We struggled with each decision because we wanted to make each choice a perfect one to honor our baby. Choosing Mass cards was a grueling task, too. There were so many beautifully written verses that seemed "fitting" for Daniel. But it was hard for us to actually read them when our eyes were brimming with tears.

After narrowing the selection down to a few, we chose "Broken Chain" written by Ron Tranmer, which seemed so appropriate for our Lucky Link:

Broken Chain

We little knew that morning, God was going to call your name;
In life we loved you dearly, in death we do the same.
It broke our hearts to lose you, you did not go alone;
For part of us went with you, the day God called you home.

You left us beautiful memories, your love is still our guide;
And though we cannot see you, you are always by our side.
Our family chain is broken, and nothing seems the same;
But as God calls us one by one, the chain will link again.

Daniel's Mass of the Angels for Children took place on Wednesday, June 2nd, and it was a beautifully special tribute to our precious son. We were surrounded and embraced by the love and sympathy of friends and family. It was such sweet evidence that Daniel's reach was far and wide. I remember walking into the church and being bombarded with grieving faces. People were coming at us left and right to offer us hugs and express their condolences. It seemed like our job was to console everyone – not in a bad way – but Jimmy and I knew that the wounds were still so fresh for them, while God had somewhat prepared us in advance for this frightening reality. Some in attendance chose to fade into the background as if the mere idea of our agony was far too painful for them to bear. Perhaps they were afraid that they would explode into tears if they approached us.

Daniel's cousins, Murphy and Myles (who were fourteen and twelve at the time), graciously accepted our request to be pall bearers along with their Father David, Matt, and my brother Andrew. It was so tough on all of them – we knew – but they selflessly, with tears in their eyes, walked beside Daniel's casket, so proud and honored to be a part of this tribute to his short life. A large picture of Daniel (taken by Aunt Sheila on Easter Sunday) was placed on an easel near the altar and by his casket. The expression on his face was so jubilant that it was difficult not to smile even as we cried at the same time.

Picture of Daniel from Easter Sunday

Deacon Lee eulogized Daniel so beautifully – sharing stories about how his life – and his death – had positively affected so many adults as well as so many children in the church school. Deacon Lee talked about Daniel's mission here on Earth and how – though it didn't probably make sense to anyone present – God had a purpose and a plan for him. We had heard that someone thought to bring a large bag filled with packages of tissues and then passed them out to those who needed them. Not surprisingly, there weren't many dry eyes in the church pews that day.

Aixa, Hannah's mother, took charge of arranging the flowers for us. Jimmy and I chose red, which we believe (through the various clothing and toy choices he'd made) was Daniel's favorite color, and red – the color of Pentecost – symbolizes the Holy Spirit. Then we chose white to represent Daniel's purity, and purple to represent mourning. The arrangements were simple and stunning.

Our parish musical director, Bill, along with Doug – a baritone from a neighboring parish – graciously donated their beautiful God-given talents to us and really made Daniel's funeral Mass extra special. We are forever grateful. Their music selections were perfect. The Holy Spirit had prompted me to call our friend, Noreen, on Tuesday to ask if she thought her daughter, Bridget, would be willing to sing at Daniel's funeral. Noreen called me right back to report that Bridget would be honored. I had only one personal musical request, and it was a song called "We Are One Body, One Body in Christ." As fate would have it, Bridget not only knew the song well, she had sung it at school, and she performed it beautifully at Daniel's Mass. For weeks after the funeral, that song echoed in my head. It became my anthem and provided me with solace whenever the agonizing panic of reality and loss would set in.

The most memorable part of Daniel's funeral for me was the overwhelming contradiction of needing to selfishly mourn for *our* loss, but at the same time, wanting to glorify Jesus Christ for blessing us with Daniel in the first place. Our delicate balancing act of grief and gratitude felt like teetering at the dead center of a seesaw. Nothing about our harrowing experience made sense to us as humans, yet everything made sense from our faith perspective – so much loss, yet such a greater gain with eternal life. And so, in our darkest hours, Jimmy and I praised the Lord for the precious gift of Daniel.

Our family knew that much of our parish community had been praying for Daniel, and we found out that the entire school had been praying for him, as well. Jimmy and I had no idea how many people would attend our son's funeral, but we guessed that it would be a lot. We knew Daniel had affected many, and we just wanted to be able to thank everyone who had made our baby such a priority in their prayers. My husband and I were both concerned because there was no way we would be able to accommodate enough people at our house after Daniel's funeral, so the church was kind enough to allow us to host a memorial reception at their family life center immediately following Daniel's funeral. Close friends (and some acquaintances, even) corresponded and worked together to provide the refreshments and all that goes with a reception so that our family didn't need to worry over one single detail.

That was where and when I delivered a completely unplanned and unrehearsed faith-guided eulogy. Given my phobia of public speaking, it could have only been the Grace of God that allowed me to easily and calmly deliver His message of faith that day. Thanking the crowd for coming to honor Daniel, I first needed to acknowledge that he had been everybody's baby, simply because he was. Daniel truly belonged to all of us – our family, our friends, our community, the world that we know. He had gently and genuinely touched all of us. Those who'd only met Daniel once or twice immediately recognized a certain brightness and wisdom about him. Quite honestly, he was openly loved and cherished by all. Even people who'd never met him – but had read about his struggle through the blog (which followed his every move) – prayed for him. Daniel belonged to them as well. On the day of his funeral, we truly knew that everyone's heart ached right along with ours. Every single one of us felt the sting of losing Daniel.

During that spontaneous eulogy, I also shared an earlier life-changing moment in faith. This story was about our friends Dana and Steve who, in 2004, lost their six year old son, Stephen, to leukemia. It had been a valiant battle, but Stephen was – sadly – destined to move on. I remember arriving at his funeral and seeing hundreds of people sobbing. Some were having trouble holding themselves together, while others were having trouble simply holding themselves up.

Then there was Dana, Stephen's remarkable mother, who approached the altar and proceeded to speak the most comforting, eloquent and faith-filled words to all of us. Her serenity and grace soothed the hundreds of people in attendance, and I remember watching her in sheer awe.

"How can she possibly be so strong?" I asked myself. The answer was clear – only by the Grace of God. I truly believe that at that moment, Dana was divinely embraced, and she spoke flawlessly about her faith and her son's illness. She told us that her job as a mother was to do what was right and necessary for her son, and watching him suffer uselessly was simply not an option. So she surrendered her little boy and watched him go to Heaven.

I know that Dana's faith and compassion changed my life – and many other lives, as well – on that day. After witnessing Stephen's passing at the hospital (when Dana and Steve had to unplug him from the life-support system), one of our mutual friends even converted from Judaism to Catholicism. Stephen's funeral was, in fact, the day that I (and several others whom I know) decided to find a permanent church home. I longed for that same type of a relationship with God – with Jesus Christ. I wanted the same sort of unwavering and profound faith that could get someone through absolutely anything, no matter how awful or painful, just as I had witnessed through Dana. That family's painful experience sent us on a mission – one that resulted in a true faith transformation when Jimmy and I found our home and entered the Catholic faith through the Rite of Christian Initiation for Adults (RCIA) program at St. Vincent Ferrer Catholic Church in 2006.

Stephen's funeral was also the day when I knew in my heart that I simply had to be a mother. Despite the toughest loss imaginable, I could see right through Dana's pain to the unconditional, selfless love that she had for her son. So, at the ripe age of thirty-seven, I finally began to realize that I longed for that relationship with a child, too, which planted the seed for our first adoption. We will always be grateful to Dana and her family for sharing their love story with us.

Fast forward six years. It seems surreal that now I am that mother saddened by the loss of her son. But I am also, miraculously, the mother who is divinely embraced and strengthened by faith. Maybe God brought us to Dana and her family in order to prepare us for our future – a shared and similar journey of selfless love for our children and for God. Today, our family is inspired and humbled by the fact that our sweet son, Daniel, touched so many people in such a short time and that his story, like Stephen's, has similarly brought many people back to their faith.

On the afternoon of Daniel's funeral, an ominous thunderstorm broke out, and when it cleared, the skies turned bright blue, and then the most bold and beautiful double rainbow formed in the sky. Madi and a few of her little friends ran outside, jumped up and down in our yard, and chanted, "DANIEL! DANIEL!" I couldn't remember the last time I'd seen a rainbow, especially one so vibrant, and it was such a beautiful gift from God that day. It was impossible not to feel His presence at that time.

We began to receive countless supportive emails and blog posts from friends (and even from total strangers) about how Daniel's story had touched them and their families. We were blessed with messages about how his story had helped people reexamine their faith and head back to God. Daniel's life – and death – had opened hearts and caused a spiritual reawakening among many. He was a little lamb who, with great purpose, led a flock back to our Lord in a very short time. Hundreds of comforting sympathy cards, Masses dedicated to Daniel, and enrollments of spiritual healing were sent to our family. We even received sympathy cards from some of the doctors and nurses who had cared for Daniel at the hospital in Miami. They, too, had been devastated by our loss.

And as friends and community came together, we received even more blessings: We discovered that the night when Hannah had babysat Daniel, she had managed to capture, in one short evening, a wide variety of sweet and candid pictures of Daniel doing his favorite things – swinging and sliding in our own backyard. Some of these photos were posted on a board at Daniel's Mass reception. This adorable close-up of Daniel was also taken by Hannah and given to us when he was in the hospital. Jimmy and I had taken it down to Miami, and it was hanging on Daniel's door. The nurses had all commented how much they appreciated seeing that picture every day. It was such a departure from the poor baby so quietly resting in a medically-induced coma while hooked up to a million beeping machines. As you can imagine, those photos from Hannah are now like gold to us. We had no idea they'd even existed.

Photo of Daniel by Hannah

Shortly after Daniel's passing, I had a revelation and remembered that we had taken videotape footage! I cannot explain what a profound blessing these tapes are. It's like they brought (and continue to bring) Daniel back to life, and they continually allow us to, once again, see him in action. We have unbelievable footage of our time together in China, including the first moments when Daniel was placed in our arms. We had taped the entire trip with him, and I had also managed to take hours of precious film chronicling our brief but blessed months with him home. I am almost always guaranteed to be behind the camera giving typically loud narration, but there are so many treasured moments of Jimmy dancing with the kids, footage with various friends and family members, Daniel in the backyard, Valentine's Day, Easter, etc., etc.

Perhaps the most precious footage is of Madi feeding Daniel. After her brother passed away, one of Madi's saddest moments was when she declared that she "never got to feed Daniel." Well, this videotape footage certainly proved otherwise! We had forgotten that, one day in the spring, she and Daniel had shared about twenty beautiful and fun-filled minutes of feeding time together. It had been a couple of months since Daniel had rejected his highchair, but on that particular day, Daniel just decided to climb into his highchair and allowed Madi to totally baby him. He loved every minute of it, and so did his big sister. It was so out of character for Daniel's "big boy" mannerisms, which made it such an extra blessing to capture that priceless footage of the two of them.

Just days after Daniel's funeral, I remembered that our St. Vincent Ferrer Bible Camp was taking place the next week. For several years prior, I had taken a leadership position of some sort in the camp but had declined participation months before Daniel's surgery knowing that his post-op care might be too much to add to the schedule-juggling mix. But, given the unexpected circumstances, I realized that Madi could use a bit of normalcy, and quite frankly, so could I. It still amazes me that – miraculously – there were only two spots open: one for a camper, and one for a leader. It was as if the Holy Spirit knew that my daughter and I needed to do this together, so he created an opening for both of us. The theme of the camp that year was "The Spirit of the Seas," and Noah's Ark – and the rainbow after the storm – were part of those lessons. No wonder why the Holy Spirit made a way for our attendance – we needed that message more than we even knew.

Perhaps one of the most meaningful gestures following Daniel's departure came from a co-worker of Jimmy's. He and his family became a secret group of princesses and began sending surprise care packages to Madi. They knew that these gifts wouldn't take away Madi's pain, but the "Petro Princesses" wanted to give our four-year old daughter some joy – the joy that perhaps her grieving parents would have a difficult time focusing on. Their gifts made her so happy, which made our hearts overflow as well. The princesses were so largely embraced by Madi that they continued to shower her at every single holiday, and then some. Still today – though Madi's days of believing in princesses are gone – they send special gifts to our family.

Father's Day fell on June 20th that year. One can only imagine just how difficult that occasion was for my sweet husband, whose wounds were still so fresh. I know Jimmy felt extra thankful to have precious Madi by his side. We tried our best to console him and make him feel special, but despite our efforts, it was quite an emotional day for Jimmy as he mourned his son's absence on what would have been their first Father's Day together.

♡

Chapter Twenty-Six

PEACE

$\mathcal{W}e$ realized that, after things began to quiet down, we'd unintentionally left everyone hanging with the loss of Daniel. Our blog postings from the hospital had been so positive and then took such a sudden turn when Daniel's condition declined so rapidly. Jimmy and I hadn't even given our friends an explanation about what happened on that somber day. In fact, we didn't even have much of an understanding ourselves.

The night that Daniel died, his cardiothoracic surgeon had given us his phone number and encouraged us to call and meet with him once we felt ready. He told us that we would probably think of many questions to ask once the dust settled, and he was right. The surgeon knew we would have questions, and he knew that – since it was all such a blur – Jimmy and I would want and need more information.

We realized that some of our questions probably couldn't be answered, and we were okay with that. I don't think that "closure" is necessarily the appropriate word for what we were seeking. My husband and I hoped that learning just a few details about what had happened would give us peace, which was ultimately what we were looking for.

The night before Jimmy and I headed down to Miami to meet with Daniel's surgeon, (which was about one month after he died) we experienced so many mixed emotions. He and I had been questioned by numerous people about whether or not we had considered a lawsuit against the hospital. And some of our family members even felt it could be a sensible thing to consider. We realized that there was a lot of anger surrounding Daniel's death, and it felt wrong to both of us. Inside *our* hearts, Jimmy and I knew that this was not a problem that could be solved with money. The "blame game" wouldn't accomplish anything here, and a lawsuit wouldn't bring our son back. In fact, my husband and I felt it would probably just take away money from all those poor and abandoned babies in the hospital who needed constant care.

As Jimmy and I walked out to our backyard that evening to discuss our range of emotions about our meeting the next day, we looked up in the sky and saw yet another beautiful double rainbow. The timing was too perfect, and that rainbow instantly brought comfort to both of us. It seemed such a clear sign that everything would be okay, and that unexpected rainbow gave us immeasurable peace within.

On the morning of June 24th, Jimmy and I drove down to Miami (accompanied by Bubba) and met with Daniel's surgeon. He, thankfully, was able to provide us with a lot of the missing pieces we needed about our baby's decline, even though there are still – even today – many questions that we (and the doctors) will never have all the answers to. At least after our meeting, Jimmy and I felt that we were closer than before to understanding what had happened to Daniel. And that gave us some of the peace that we were looking for.

It seemed that after his corrective surgery had taken place, Daniel's lungs just couldn't adjust. Although the heart surgery was a success, evidently our son's heart and lungs weren't used to the pulsations and pressures that resulted from his new and improved heart function. Daniel's lungs began to fill with fluid, but not at an alarming rate. In fact, the x-ray they took at 3:00 a.m. on the morning after his operation was not worrisome. Even the blood gas tests were not alarming until about 6:00 a.m. In hindsight, Daniel likely had a pulmonary hemorrhage that filled his lungs with blood in addition to the fluid that was already there. This made it more difficult for Daniel to breathe and resulted in his cardiac arrest at 8:00 a.m.

Could they have done things differently? Perhaps. Maybe they could have waited longer to extubate him, or maybe they could have put a breathing tube back in with the first signs of deterioration. But again – there had been nothing alarming to indicate that it was imperative to do so at that particular time.

Daniel's immediate and official cause of death was abdominal sepsis. On top of all of his other organ issues and failures, his intestines suffered one of two problems. He either had an intestinal perforation or else part of his intestine had become gangrenous and then ruptured. We will never know which one actually occurred since we declined an autopsy, but it was quite obvious that the increased swelling in his abdomen on Saturday (and into the night) was very serious. And it sent Daniel into cardiac arrest for the second time in his short life.

The doctors had seen an abdominal issue approaching, and they even performed tests to pinpoint the problem, but we were told that the intestines are kind of a "dark horse" in the medical field. Surprisingly, there aren't many ways to detect those problems early on, he said, and since they also progress very quickly, the only solution to this problem would have been emergency surgery. Jimmy and I (and the doctors) are not so sure that Daniel's tired little body would have made it through the surgery. He was still on a ventilator, kidney dialysis, and heart pacing monitors. It would have been an uphill battle for sure, and it would have meant going back on the ECMO machine, more anesthesia, etc., etc. We believe that the Good Lord gave Daniel the easy way out – a ticket to Heaven.

Daniel's surgeon was very "human" that day. Jimmy and I feared that – given Daniel's outcome – he might be on the defensive, but that wasn't the case. He explained that every human anatomy is different and that the exact same surgery performed on ten different bodies could result in ten totally different outcomes. He answered our questions honestly, thoughtfully, and very professionally. My husband and I (and Bubba, too) found our longed-for peace from attaining knowledge about Daniel's condition, even knowing that different steps in his treatment may or may not have affected his outcome. We will never know. The fact of the matter is that his doctors are people. Not mind readers. And they are not perfect; they are only human. We watched them give Daniel everything they could, and we felt *their pain* from losing him.

The deepest peace we received came from the answer to our most important question. Jimmy and I wanted to know if they'd learned anything – if not multiple lessons – from Daniel's case that might save the life or lives of future children. Fortunately, the answer was "Yes." They had learned enough to enable them to already make changes in both their procedures and their thinking patterns. The staff members who knew Daniel and loved him promised us (and Daniel) that his death had not been in vain. Our son left a legacy at that hospital that *will* make a difference.

Of course, something like this doesn't happen without guilt – and questions – coming into play. Jimmy and I began to struggle with so many things: Had we chosen the wrong hospital? Had we operated too soon? Should we not have operated at all? These were all completely normal thoughts and questions, and we beat ourselves up (for months) wondering if we could have changed this heartbreaking outcome. I also wished that we had at least taken Daniel for a second opinion to another well known hospital in Miami that also specializes in pediatric heart surgeries. And for months after we lost him, I beat myself up about our choices – repeatedly wondering if it would have made a difference. I imagine that I would have carried tremendous guilt had we gone through the same process somewhere else and ended up with the same result of losing Daniel, especially if I had been solely responsible for pushing to use a different hospital and another surgeon. Obviously, our family will never know what the outcome would have been had that happened.

Jimmy and I spent countless nights in bed crying in each other's arms, talking each other through the pain and anguish. And we had to constantly remind ourselves of something that we already knew, but had temporarily lost sight of – *our faith*. If we truly believe in God's plan and trust that everything happens according to His will, then we *must* acknowledge that we are not in control – God is. We had followed His every sign each step of the way. This outcome would have happened *no matter what*. We *were chosen* as Daniel's parents for a reason, and Daniel *was given* to us for a reason. Jimmy and I knew all of this; we just had to push doubt away and wholeheartedly embrace the everlasting truth of God's word. And every time we did, our sadness and guilt were washed away and replaced by faith.

On Friday, June 26th, twenty-four days after his funeral, we laid Daniel's ashes to rest. Jimmy and I chose the Mausoleum in Boca Raton where his grandparents are buried; his Uncle Bill's ashes are also there. Grandpa Murphy had never laid Grandma Pauline's ashes to rest when she passed, so we appropriately placed Daniel's urn in the same niche with Grandma Pauline's urn. Their ashes here on

Earth are together, and they are in Heaven together, as well. There had been much discussion about where to put both their ashes. While my mind was initially set on burying them, Madi would have nothing to do with that idea and insisted that Daniel's ashes be put in the wall where they would "be safe." We then learned (from Grandpa) that Grandma Pauline had had no desire to be buried in the ground either, so we complied with Madi's wishes.

Deacon Lee, once again, graced us with a very special graveside service honoring both Daniel and Grandma Pauline. As Deacon Lee eulogized them, a soft, cool breeze picked up out of nowhere and continued on until he was through. And I'm not kidding! Five minutes later, the air was so thick and still you could have sliced it with a knife. It seemed like another message from the Holy Spirit sent to let us know that Daniel and Grandma had both safely arrived Home.

Chapter Twenty-Seven

LITTLE LAMB DAN

It was truly inspiring to realize how Daniel's life (and death) had touched so many other children. His journey had been followed by the entire student body at St. Vincent's School. After Daniel passed away, the school's religion teacher, Miss Ann, approached us at Mass with tear-filled eyes and thanked us for sharing our son with the school.

Miss Ann told us how his story had sparked so much discussion about faith, God's will, hope, and salvation. It was obviously difficult for the children to comprehend how serious illness and death could happen to a two-year-old child, and Daniel's story allowed them to see the hope of salvation close up. Miss Ann reminded us that we had done the ultimate job as parents: "to get our children to Heaven." Jimmy and I had never thought of our experience that way, and it was truly an enlightening perspective of faith.

Daniel and Madi's cousin, Matthew, who lives in New Hampshire and was seven years old at the time, was in such a state of anger and disbelief that he told my brother, Andrew, "Daddy, I think Mary should punish Jesus for taking Daniel!" Matthew was truly sad and angry that he had been denied the chance to meet his cousin in person.

Julianna and Jonathon (Matt and Sherril's children), who were both quite involved with Daniel during his short time with us, reacted so differently – as each child does. Jonathon, who was eleven at the time, never faltered from his faith and even comforted other children by explaining that Daniel simply "took off his coat" so that he could go to Heaven to be with Jesus. Jonathon was very sad, but he was comfortable with the fact that Daniel was truly in a better place. He actually handled it better than some of us adults! In fact, he handled it so well that we asked him to do a reading at the funeral. Jonathon graciously accepted and honored Daniel in a truly special way by doing so.

Julianna, on the other hand, was blatantly devastated. She was nine years old and had shared a special bond with Daniel. In fact, she had been able to get reactions from him like no one else. He would roll around on the floor in her presence. Whenever Julianna left our house, Daniel would beat on the glass storm door and demand extra hugs and kisses from her. He adored Jules, and she just couldn't accept that he was gone. Jimmy and I gave her some of Daniel's things to comfort her (a pillow and one of his blankets), and she is adamant that someday she will name a son of her own *Daniel*.

Shortly after Daniel passed away, Julianna had a dream about him. Her description was so sweet that it brought tears to my eyes. She said that he looked the same and had a huge smile on his face. Julianna also said that Daniel's eyes looked really big and very bright, and she woke up feeling differently after having that dream. We were so happy for her because she was really struggling. I asked her to tell Daniel – in her next dream – to please come home to his Mommy. He hadn't yet returned to me in a dream.

Kids can be so wise beyond their years when it comes to faith. Madi, for example, has been so incredibly strong. We talk about Daniel all the time and cherish all the funny moments we shared together. Whenever we see butterflies or dragonflies, we chase them and sometimes swear that they are Daniel and Grandma checking in on us. Jimmy and I are not worried about our daughter. She is at such peace with the fact that Daniel is with Grandma and with Jesus in Heaven.

Every night at dinner after his passing, Madi would set up a little shrine of Daniel for our centerpiece. And when we would say grace, we would hold hands and leave a space open where Daniel's hands would have been. Sometimes, Madi and I would dance in the kitchen as they had done so frequently together. As she played her Fridge D.J. (a little musical toy on our refrigerator), we would put our hands to our knees and rock up and down. We both remembered Daniel doing that dance, and we laughed as we read each other's minds. I love that we didn't have to say a word – we just shared that special moment. That is how we always want to remember Daniel.

We receive an occasional message about something a child has said in his or her infinite wisdom. In order to console her mother, Carmen, as she struggled with the loss of Daniel one day, Madi's friend Ami Mei said, "Mom, he will *always* live in our hearts."

Our dear friends, Michelle and Dave, honored Daniel with a beautiful memorial plaque for our yard, and Dave installed it in our backyard butterfly garden. It serves as such a sweet reminder of Daniel playing in his favorite place, his backyard. Sometimes, Jimmy and I look at that infant swing swaying in the wind, and we can almost picture Daniel sitting in there with the squinty expression he used to get when the sun was shining brightly. We can almost hear him shouting, "My turn, my turn" in that sweet little Chinese tone whenever Daddy would take turns pushing him and Madi in their swings.

We received so many heartwarming notices of donations made to charities in Daniel's name. Before his funeral, we chose three charities that were close to our hearts. The first, People in Crisis United (www.peopleincrisisunited.org) was an organization founded by one of the nurses at the children's hospital to provide for the children in P.I.C.U. Most of them didn't have much of anything. As I mentioned, some of them didn't even have families. People in Crisis United was formed to help give those kids something to look forward to – an experience they may never have a chance to receive, a special toy to bring them joy, or items to simply meet their needs.

We also chose the Ronald McDonald House Charities (www.rmhcsouthflorida.org) since it was clear to see that they do so much good for families who otherwise would not be able to be close with their loved ones while in the hospital. And they had certainly done a lot for us. On the day that Daniel passed away, Jimmy and I called the Ronald McDonald House to let them know about our son and to notify them that we would not be back. When we inquired about payment, the manager revealed that our entire bill was less than $300 for our twenty-day stay. Jimmy and I couldn't imagine what a hotel bill would have added up to for the same duration. The Ronald McDonald House had been a tremendous blessing.

We began collecting aluminum pop tabs for the Ronald McDonald House Charities, too. They recycle the pop tabs and then use the money to help run their facilities. This fundraising effort has become a great way for the kids to get involved and make a difference without having to give money or ask people for donations. Not a beer or soda can get by Madi without her snagging the pop tab. Bubba and I made a trip to one of the locations with Madi and Julianna to deliver a large bag of pop-tabs last summer. With the generous support of Madi's preschool director, Peggie, we started an initiative at her school last year, and many families contributed. Accompanied by several of Madi's friends, she and I delivered another good-sized contribution to the Ronald McDonald House at the end of the 2010/2011 school year. In fact, the preschool (and church) continue to collect them, and we will likely continue this charitable effort for our lifetime. We still – from time to time – hear from friends who tell us how their children continue to collect pop tabs for Daniel.

The charity choice that was probably nearest and dearest to our hearts was Half the Sky Foundation (www.halfthesky.org), since they had done so much for Daniel as a baby. I noticed that one of my dearest friends and her husband had donated to Half the Sky's "Heart Project" in Daniel's name, and I hadn't even heard of this before. As I scanned their website for more information, I found the link to their special heart-focused program, which provided heart surgeries for orphans, and I remember feeling so angry when I made this discovery. Why hadn't Daniel been a recipient? Why hadn't our son been one of those lucky babies to receive a life-saving heart surgery when he was an infant?

We'll never know the answer to that question. It certainly wasn't Half the Sky's fault. Maybe Jimmy and I would have never known Daniel if that had happened. Perhaps we would never have had the chance to love him. But this discovery prompted me to call Half the Sky Foundation and ask if we could request all donations made in Daniel's name to be allocated to their heart project. They agreed, and I felt an overwhelming sense of peace knowing that another child's life might be saved thanks to the generous donations made by friends and family in Daniel's name.

Chapter Twenty-Eight

TOUCHED BY AN ANGEL

$\mathcal{D}aniel$ touched many lives, but he *really* had an impact on Amanda, one of his anesthesiologists at the children's hospital in Miami. Amanda is a medical professional who truly deserves her own chapter.

In the medical world, they say that medicine and emotions shouldn't mix, but Amanda broke all the rules. She happily allowed her heart – as well as her faith – to get involved. Her bond with Daniel was strong as steel from the first day we met her, which was before his catheter procedure. She was kind and loving with him while being consistently compassionate with us. Amanda professes to be Daniel's second love (after Julianna, of course). It is amazing how God puts different people in our paths for different reasons. Her experience with Daniel has now changed her life in significant ways.

When Amanda found out (through our blog) that Daniel had died, she went ballistic. She went to the hospital that Monday morning in a fit of rage. She wanted two things: answers and somebody to blame. She searched and searched for both, but couldn't come up with anything except the realization, through faith, that God simply needed Daniel.

When our family entered the picture, Amanda was unsure about the direction of her future medical career. She was finishing up her internship and preparing to take her boards but wasn't sure whether to stay in pediatric anesthesiology or switch to adult anesthesiology. Meeting Daniel influenced her decision to stick with pediatrics. Although losing Daniel caused her to once again question her choices, she received multiple indications from our Holy Spirit that pediatrics is where she was meant to stay. We couldn't agree more.

Amanda returned from completing a fellowship in Boston at Boston Children's Hospital, and she passed her board exams in 2011. She claims that she passed her exams "because of Daniel," and felt his presence during the entire process. She had arrived in Utah where the exams – her final step to becoming a Board Certified Anesthesiologist – took place. As she sat in her hotel room praying to pass her exams, she decided to order room service. Amanda, who *never* reads a newspaper, decided to open up the newspaper that was delivered that morning on her room service tray. The article on the cover jumped into her face, and she believed Daniel was giving her a sign that everything would be okay. The article on the front page was called "It's a Matter of Heart," and it was all about life-saving heart surgeries.

Amanda accepted the post as Assistant Professor of Anesthesiology (specializing in pediatric cardiac anesthesia) in the very children's hospital where she had cared for Daniel less than two years before. Jimmy and I know that Amanda will now be in our lives forever. The bond our family forged with her is beyond words. We are forever grateful to Amanda for the way she loved Daniel and gave him such exceptional care. Hers was the last face he saw as well as the last voice he heard before his surgery took place, and that is a very, very comforting thought for us. We pray that Amanda will continue to answer the call she's been given and have a positive impact on the lives of many, many children in the future.

This is an email Amanda sent to us on the day after Daniel's funeral Mass:

Dear Lisa, Jim, Madi (and the rest of the Murphy family),

Getting your message the next morning warmed my heart as much because of your extremely kind words as it was that I had so many things to say to you at the Mass, but did not want to monopolize your precious time with so many of your loved ones also wanting to spend time with you. First of all, I want to apologize to you. I made the distressing discovery on Sunday morning at 0830 a.m. when I woke up. Like I had done every morning since you had given me the site, I would check the blog first thing in the morning (and then several times a day thereafter) any day that I knew I would not be there to look in on Daniel in person. When I read the title and saw the photos, I knew something had happened, but I was unable to comprehend the words on the page for what felt like an eternity. I woke up my boyfriend and made him read the blog too, as I was sure I did not understand. Entirely overcome with feelings of sadness, confusion, grief, defeat, and loss, I could not conjure up a single coherent thought. My heart broke for your family.

At that moment I thought about running to the hospital, but made the sad realization that none of you would be there. I then realized that the only method of communication I had with you was the blog and I spent all of Sunday and Monday trying to think of something to say there that would accurately express how I felt, but every time I tried the words seemed so inadequate. I contemplated searching the medical record for a telephone number, but knew it was a breach of privacy and did not want to inadvertently offend you. So I said nothing and for that I apologize. I hoped and prayed that you would post the info for his memorial on the blog and you did. Once again, the Holy Spirit at work.

Secondly, I spent much of these last few days trying to figure out what happened. I thought knowing would be some consolation to myself and might help me answer any questions you might have had. The more I looked, the more I came up empty-handed. And it was at that moment that I realized, this was God's will and in that I took (some) solace. God called him and he went just like he was supposed to. I just kept reading your entry that said we prayed him right home to Jesus. I agree with you. I think we did.

Thirdly, was a thought that occurred to me on Monday night. From the very first day I met your family, I noticed two things. The first was that being around you was like sitting by a fireplace... it gave me the warm and fuzzies. It seemed like all the good stuff in life got rolled into this family named Murphy. The night of Daniel's catheter, I went home and told my boyfriend AND my parents AND my siblings about this family of angels on Earth. I still feel that way, now more than ever and it explains why just being around you guys feels so wonderful. The second thing was a little harder to explain though... From that very first day, you both were eerily familiar. It was strangely comfortable and worn in...

Until now, I still don't know what it is, perhaps, we have met before, or perhaps, it is that we are united in Christ.

Whatever the reason, it is a good feeling, and one that I enjoyed being around. And so as I was getting ready for work the next morning, it dawned on me that not only was my precious Daniel not going to be there, but neither you nor any of your phenomenal family and friends would be either. And again, an enormous sense of loss overcame me.

Somewhere, in all of this, you all stopped being my patient/patient family, and became my friends. Not only had I lost my dear patient, but also the company of people who made everyone around them better for having known them. Each one of you has this incredible ability to make the people around you feel good. I found it strangely ironic that you would tell me that the Holy Spirit sent me to you. What I will NEVER be able to explain to you is that you all miraculously waltzed into my life at a time when I felt very low, and I was questioning my faith in everything especially, love and God. And so, I think you have it backwards Murphy family, I think the Holy Spirit sent you to help ME. So again, please don't thank me. It is I who needs to thank you. (It was yet another intervention by the Holy Spirit that the Mass was Wednesday... if it had been any other day, I would not have been able to go... so for that I am grateful.)

In addition, Daniel's picture is on my desk. Every time I see it, I feel sad, but then after a little while, I think of him looking drunk before surgery or playing with my stethoscope and it makes me smile. I will NEVER EVER EVER be able to express to you how just bearing witness to your faith through what I know were some of the darkest times, and feeling the love that you have for each other and all around you has rekindled my faith in the Greatness of God, and the power of love. I feel so fortunate to have been able to take care of Daniel for some part of the time he was here on Earth and for the privilege of meeting each of you. It is an experience that has changed me forever and one I won't ever forget. Finally, I still check the blog... everyday... and I have a feeling that I always will. :) I too would love to keep in touch. Feel free to call me or email me WHENEVER. I'm always here if you need me. Maybe one day Madi could take us on a tea date (to a quiet tea house, of course) when you guys are free and feel like getting away for a few hours. I can be in Delray in 90 minutes. God bless!

With love always!!!
Amanda

On August 4, 2010, we received another moving email from sweet Amanda:

Lisa, Jimmy, and Madi...

You guys NEVER CEASE TO AMAZE ME!!! Thank you so much. I got your email just hours before going into my test yesterday and it was so heart-warming! And yet another Murphy moment...

After I took the test, I was discouraged because it was quite difficult and I had to make educated guesses on more questions than I had wanted to. Because I'm a notoriously bad guesser, this was VERY disconcerting. As I was driving home feeling VERY low, it began to rain... Even though the sun was shining high and bright in the sky... "How odd! Well, it's just that kind of day," I thought.

I began looking up some of the answers... Many of them that I had absolutely no idea about I had gotten RIGHT! Then it happened... Out of nowhere appeared a beautiful RAINBOW! Immediately I remembered the day of Daniel's Mass... "That's DANIEL!!! He did it AGAIN! He's trying to tell me that everything is going to be alright!"

You told me he was my guardian angel and did he ever prove it yesterday! Thank you for sharing him with me yesterday! The poor little guy had his work cut out for him!!!

Love you all!
Mandy

And Daniel continues to touch Amanda's life! On September 5, 2010, Jimmy and I received an email containing this excerpt:

Fast forward to today... A hectic morning at the hospital. I was already running a little late only to walk in to find that I'd been assigned to the early start room that required a great deal of preparation which clearly I did not have time for. "FANSTINKINGTASTIC!" I thought. "A lovely way to start the week!!!" I wanted to pull my hair out.

But when I saw my patient everything was different. I was served a very large helping of perspective. My patient was a 5 year old Asian boy and to add insult to injury he had an American name. "Really? REALLY God?! I mean, SERIOUSLY?!?!" He is the first Asian patient I've had since

I'd taken care of Daniel, and quite honestly, I wasn't sure how I was going to do it...this was a moment I knew would come eventually, but honestly one I was dreading.

I managed to keep it together and when I could finally no longer see his face that was covered by the sterile drape I felt a bit relieved. And then, the most amazing thing transpired. When the surgery was over, those two little sparkly black eyes opened and smiled. NO ONE wakes up from anesthesia smiling. No one. I picked up his hand and held it and a warm tingly feeling came over me.

I always feel like Daniel is with me, and that he touches my life everyday... but today, for just one second, I felt like Daniel was there, and that I got to touch him back. I feel blessed that he showed himself to me today. I don't know why he's decided to be my angel, but I am sooo thankful for it. I say a prayer to him every night and ask him to help me make the right decisions with my patients. Maybe he came by to ask me to STOP since he's busy looking for his new brother or sister... not to mention looking out for his mother, father, sister, and the rest of his family... I'm not sure... whatever the case... I feel like I was meant to tell you that even though we can't see him or touch him like before, he still sees and touches us... every day.

Love you guys!!! – Mandy

Update: *As of this revised version, Amanda continues to receive signs from Daniel. She frequently emails us pictures of hearts she finds lying in her path!*

Chapter Twenty-Nine

THE HEALING PROCESS

The idea of moving forward seemed wrong to us. After all – Daniel couldn't move on (although he had literally "moved on" in the greatest sense of the expression!) so why should I be able move on *without him*? There was a part of me that yearned to linger in the pain and sadness forever. Even though Daniel wasn't with us physically, the painful bruise that was left behind kept me feeling close to him. It felt as if moving on with life would somehow mean forgetting what happened or neglecting to properly acknowledge our son's suffering and our loss – that if I remained in a state of anguish, then that meant I could continue to live with Daniel close to my heart.

Slowly but surely, I began to realize that Daniel would forever remain in my heart, and I could begin to let go of the pain. Carrying on was God's will – part of His plan.

I also found that I desperately wanted – and needed – to talk about Daniel, a lot, and to whomever would listen. When I met people for the first time, I felt compelled to tell them about him, too. *"Hi. My name is Lisa. I have two kids – well, one child here on earth. The other, my son Daniel, is in Heaven."*

I could almost see the panic in their eyes as they took in the news that I blurted out so matter-of-factly. It's not that I took it lightly by any stretch – but talking about Daniel kept him there – like a lit flame, and it kept him present in our lives. It's interesting how many people don't seem to understand that. So many people are afraid to bring up the name of a lost loved one – as if that might "remind" a person of his or her loss. I, myself, used to be one of those people.

Some of our close friends with children who were Daniel's age even began to have feelings of guilt and wrongly thought that maybe it would be easier for us to not be around them. The thing is, the loss is *always* there and becomes an integral part of who you are. I found it *extremely* comforting for people to bring up Daniel's name and to talk about him freely and lovingly. I still do. To this day, in fact, people will call Charlie "Daniel." And it's okay with us. We find it quite comforting that people still remember Daniel that much and that he made such an impact on them. Jimmy and I also find it quite comfortable to be around kids his age. While on those occasions we sometimes experience the sadness of milestones missed, it also allows us to get a glimpse of the things Daniel would have been doing, and it gives my husband and me joy to imagine our sweet boy in each scenario.

Daniel's possessions have become priceless treasures to us. Madi still goes to sleep listening to "Glowy," Daniel's musical seahorse that plays classical lullabies. We listen to it together every night and probably always will. "Baby Girl," Daniel's favorite stuffed animal that Madi had given to him to take to the hospital, is propped up on her shelf of priceless collectibles. It comforts Madi to know that "Baby Girl" was with Daniel when he went to Heaven. It gives us all comfort, actually, and these items still make us feel connected to him in a special way.

Madi also sleeps with Daniel's special blanket. One of the moms from Madi's preschool, Leigh Anne, made a beautiful blanket for Daniel before we traveled to China. That blanket, which was made out of *John Deere* (Jimmy's employer at the time) fabric, made the trip with us to China to bring Daniel home, and it was with him the whole time he adjusted to his new surroundings. It went to the hospital with Daniel, and the blanket was with him to the end. Now it comforts Madi, and no one will ever appreciate his possessions the way she will. She will forever treasure them, and they will always remind Madi of her sweet baby brother.

After losing him, Daniel's bedroom served as a special place to warm our hearts – a place where we could enter, breathe deeply, and fill our lungs with his soul. I remember that after he passed away, a friend had asked me what we would do with his bedroom, and she wondered if we would make it a guest room again. My answer was unequivocally, "*No* – Daniel's bedroom is still *his* bedroom." I was appalled at the very idea. Changing our son's bedroom wasn't going to make the hurt go away – nothing would. Our loss was not something that we could bury or forget about. It was like a bad, inescapable dream.

Our grief was an open door and we intended to deal with our feelings one day at a time. We knew it was okay to cry – in fact, we welcomed it. Jimmy and I wanted Madi to see that we were human and to know that it was okay for her to be sad, too. We were aware that the more we allowed ourselves to grieve, the quicker our hearts would begin to heal. And once we could see past ourselves and our own personal pain, it became clear that we had witnessed the epitome of God's love for humanity – through His giving Daniel a loving family, baptizing him with the waters of the River Jordan, and providing him with unconditional love that he so deserved while here on this earth.

I felt an overwhelming desire to be outside during the healing process, where I swear I could actually *feel* Daniel in the elements that surround us – sometimes blowing in the breeze, in the sweet melody of birds chirping, or floating up in the puffy white clouds in a clear blue sky. I felt such a strong connection to Daniel in our beautiful, natural God-given environment that I had posted about it on the blog shortly after his death.

WINGS | June 14, 2010

Daniel was absolutely fascinated with birds. He loved them. It always amazed me that for such a little guy, he could spot a bird in the sky a mile away. He would point his little index finger to the sky with such excitement. I think he was meant to have wings, and I'm sure he loves having them right now.

That is just one of the imprints that Daniel made on my heart. I never used to pay attention to nature the way I do now. I hear every bird chirping, and I find myself really listening to their beautiful songs. I notice every bird soaring up in the clouds, and I picture our little angel, Daniel. I can't help but smile.

Chapter Thirty

A NEW JOURNEY

Earlier in the book, I mentioned our desire to be a family of four, even when we (remotely) considered the possibility of losing Daniel that long, lonely night in May as we paced the cold hospital corridor. Only days after Daniel had passed, Jimmy and I already knew deep down inside – even at such a solemn and painful time – that we had a responsibility to share the love in our hearts (and in our family) with another child out there in the world who needed a family.

In retrospect, it seemed to happen so quickly. On the heels of such great suffering, how could God have possibly been tugging at our hearts to begin another adoption process? I can't explain it, but Jimmy and I both felt it. And though we continued to struggle with the conflicting emotions of our devastating loss, my husband and I knew inside that our family's journey just couldn't end with Daniel's death. It seemed that the Lord was asking more of us and that our gaping hole of grief needed to be filled with another blessing that only He could give – the miracle of another child. And if we truly wanted to glorify God, then shouldn't we open our hearts and trust His divine mercy by placing our fears in His loving heart and hands? Shouldn't we, once again, "stretch" ourselves and remain faithful to His plan and will?

Jimmy and I still were, understandably, confused about the prospect of adopting again so soon, even given the signs we'd received from the Holy Spirit. As the two of us would huddle together in bed at night, holding each other, and mourning over our recent loss, we both felt – and believed – that we were being called to bring another baby into our home. Jimmy and I felt very strongly that Daniel would want that for us and for his big sister. We didn't want people to think that we were trying to replace Daniel, because we weren't. Still, my husband and I weren't sure how our family and friends would view our sudden decision even though we both knew inside that it was one we had to make. And we continued to struggle with that – but we ultimately chose to follow the new road that God had begun to pave for us.

One June afternoon, I was folding laundry in Madi's room while she played and I quietly asked her, "Madi…do you think you'd ever want our family to have another baby?" There was a gap of silence so large that I thought perhaps she hadn't heard me. Then Madi suddenly turned around, waved her index finger at me, and in the most serious tone said, "I wanna go to China this time." I took her response as a resounding "yes" from our decisive, almost five-year-old daughter!

On June 14th, with much trepidation about how our request to our adoption agency would be received, we sent an email to Holt. We poured our hearts out to them and explained our desire to follow our hearts and go back. Though Jimmy and I were too fearful to take on another surgery at the time, we indicated that we were still perfectly willing to go through their special needs program again to adopt another "heart baby." We had so many questions for them – about starting all over again and enduring another wait, about our financial concerns, and ultimately, about facing our fear of the unknown once more. As I pushed that "send" button, Jimmy and I really weren't certain how they would feel about our request

– would they think it was too soon for us? Would they even be willing to work with us again?

My husband and I were both relieved and thankful that Holt responded to our wishes with total compassion and even revealed that they'd hoped we would consider another adoption. Their kind staff members, who had been exposed to new, unprecedented territory through our case, graciously offered to "walk through the process with us." And they truly did.

After several weeks of keeping our feelings and plans to ourselves, during a Mass we attended at St. Vincent Ferrer, the message we received was so clear that Jimmy and I knew it was time to move forward, so I posted about it.

A NEW JOURNEY | June 27, 2010

Today's Mass was about journeys. Moving forward in this life and following Jesus along the way. I found it a very fitting time to write this post. Days after Daniel passed away, we knew in our hearts that we wanted another child. We know that we can't replace Daniel - nor would we want to. Daniel was a very special child who left a mark on us that we will carry forever--a mark of hope, a mark of love, a mark of faith. We are better people because of him. We do feel very strongly that we have the love to give to another child, and we believe Daniel would want that for us. We know that he will be watching over us for the rest of our lives.

And so, we have begun the process to adopt again. Our path seems to be taking us back to China, back to bring another special needs child home to share common roots and heritage with big sister Madi. It will take time to go through the rigorous paperwork and waiting game, but we have the support of our kind and wonderful social worker and of our adoption agency. They have been very gracious and understanding with our situation.

It seemed insane to have to start from square one again – the dossier (paperwork), the background checks, the medical exams, the approvals, the wait, etc., etc. At first, accomplishing this painstaking task seemed like moving mountains. But we had angels. And wherever humanly possible, people seemed to step up to expedite the process and make this new dream come true for us.

Amy (our case worker) showed up at our home within a week to conduct our home study interviews. Dr. Bradford, our pediatrician, not only provided adoption physicals for Jimmy and me within days – but he never even billed us for them and had them notarized free of charge. Our neighbor and friend, Carol – for the third time – hustled to notarize all of our dossier documents in short time. As he had done with both our prior adoptions, our FedEx delivery man, Gregg, paid extra-special attention to our packages and even tracked us down on the phone when he suspected that an envelope contained adoption paperwork. Our USCIS case worker, Matthew, turned over documents and approvals within hours of their arrival to his office. And, of course, the whole staff at Holt was amazing. They did everything in their power to quickly process our dossier. And in a "protective" kind of way, it was evident how much they really cared about our case. They were nothing short of determined to find another perfect match for our family.

In November, 2010, our amazing friends, family, and community hosted a benefit fundraiser for us. Before that, Jimmy and I never realized quite how many supporters we had. I think we must be the luckiest, most blessed people on earth. We had been told several months earlier to save the date and that a babysitter would be arranged for Madi. Jimmy and I knew that a few friends had something up their sleeves because we had been given strict instructions to be ready to leave by 5:30 p.m. Our friends, Clare and Ed, came down from the Tampa area on Friday with their daughter Emily (Madi's soul mate) to be there with us, and they kept us sane on Saturday as we waited and wondered what would happen that evening. At 5:30 p.m. sharp, we drove over to Matt and Sherril's house to drop off Madi and Emily with Julianna and the sitter and to pick up Matt.

Julianna came out to the car and handed me a green rubber bracelet (like Lance Armstrong's yellow Livestrong bands) and said, "Lisa...this is your ticket to get in tonight." I read the band, and then I lost it. It read, "Think of Daniel." At that very moment, I knew it was going to be a night to remember. Before we drove away, we took a few pictures outside and then Julianna handed me a card, which we were instructed to read:

Dear Lisa and Jimmy,
Hope you have a wonderful night tonight. Can't wait to share
all of the stories leading up to this special night. Your family
is so loved — just wait and see!"

Matt guided us to the venue, which turned out to be a local Irish Pub called Finnegan's. Could there be a more appropriate place for an Irish celebration? We immediately began to grasp the full beauty of our surprise when we first saw Murphy and Myles behind a registration table. We walked up and were greeted by so many good friends. We saw a basket of those green bracelets on the table, and there were rolls of raffle tickets everywhere. Then someone handed me a postcard, and the purpose of the evening was finally revealed to us. It was a surprise celebration and fundraiser to help Daniel send his family back to China. As Jimmy and I read the postcard together, it was so mind-boggling to us – so completely beyond our comprehension – that our friends, our family, and our community would do something so utterly amazing on our behalf. It became apparent that the gift of Daniel just keeps on giving.

The night was simply unbelievable. Every moment was a surprise because every time we turned around, someone else whom we didn't expect to see was there. Friends had come together to donate silent auction and raffle items, purchase raffle tickets, and – amazingly to us – over one hundred people showed up to support our family and demonstrate their love for Daniel. Ultimately, our friends had raised a significant – and totally unexpected – amount of money to help the Murphy family of South Florida bring another precious child home from China.

Chapter Thirty-One

CHARLIE

Graced with the reward of God's plan in His timing (not ours), we received an unexpected call from Beth (at our adoption agency) on Saturday, October 23rd, 2010. It had been only five months since Daniel passed away. Even before I answered our phone and heard her voice, my heart began to pound when I saw Holt's number on the caller ID. Beth proceeded to tell us about the file of Zheng Chuan Qian, a beautiful one-year-old boy from Shanghai with a small hole in his heart (Atrial Septal Defect/ASD). Beth said that she knew the minute she came across the file that this was "The Murphy's baby."

The file, which must've been "locked" for some time by another agency, had mysteriously been "unlocked" that morning, and it was a total accident for her to find his file in the photo listings. But of course, Jimmy and I don't believe in accidents.

As Beth gave us the details about him over the phone, I could feel the familiar sting of tears when she revealed his birthday to us. He'd been born on September 16th – Grandma Pauline's birthday, which was all we needed to hear. We had been filled with so many questions about our decision to adopt again, and now the Holy Spirit had given us a loud and clear sign that we were on the right path, and that – without a doubt – this was, indeed, our baby. Grandma's bell in the backyard began ringing double-time, once again, as we dove head-first into our new adoption process.

We decided to name our son Charles Stanley Chuanqian Murphy, after both his maternal Grandfathers, and we kept his Chinese name, too. We had learned that Charlie's Chinese name, *Chuan* means "to deliver" and *Qian* means "wealth." Initially, I thought a name centered around money seemed shallow until I read further into the translation. He had been given that name by the orphanage in hopes that someday he would come into wealth and provide help to those who are in need.

When I realized the true intention of his name, it was almost breathtaking to me. What a simply beautiful name in meaning, especially since so many good people had poured out their generosity to help bring him into our family. We, too, hope and pray for such a charitable, pay-it-forward spirit in our son's future.

Since Shanghai was a province that we hadn't traveled to before, we were very curious to know more about where Charlie was from. The only piece of his past that we knew was that on December 6th, 2009, he was found by the Zhijiang West Road Police Station in Shanghai and was sent to the Children's Welfare Institute. Upon admission, he was diagnosed with an upper respiratory infection and later diagnosed with an ASD (Atrial Septal Defect) or more commonly known as a hole in his heart.

As I further researched the Shanghai Children's Welfare Institute (where Charlie was living when we received his file), we learned that its predecessor was a baby care center established by Catholic Church Union in 1911, which was very interesting to us because we are Catholic. In 1956, its name was changed to Shanghai Children's Welfare Institute.

In addition to being an orphanage, this charitable social welfare institution is also responsible for the rehabilitation of local children who have disabilities and deformities, and it also provides family care services. Charlie was one of a reported 500+ children residing there, and though we had heard that he was "lucky" to be living in such a wealthy institution (because of local support), we were prepared for physical and emotional delays – simply because of the number of children as well as the lack of constant one-on-one care and attention.

We emailed Charlie's file to both the cardiologist and cardiothoracic surgeon whom we had trusted with Daniel's file and, based on Charlie's size, they were both more concerned with his development than with his heart condition. His Atrial Septal Defect (ASD) was small, and they tend to close spontaneously. Charlie's file indicated that he was small and "under" the growth charts (both Chinese and American) in development, so we knew right away that nutrition would play a major role in getting him up to speed physically. We also knew – from personal experience – *what love alone can do for a child.*

Thanks to the suggestion of a friend, we also sent Charlie's file to the University of Minnesota's International Adoption Medicine Program & Clinic for review. We had no idea that this program even existed, and they provide an incredible service in exchange for donations. It was such a Godsend, and we were so relieved to receive this optimistic report from them about Charlie's condition:

Dear Lisa and James:

Thanks for sending Chuan Qian's records for review. He's a lovely little boy who appears to be doing reasonably well. His growth is marginal for his given age. However, since they estimated his birthday, and we don't know his birth weight or gestational age, his growth could be completely appropriate for his actual age. His update in November puts him slightly below or at the lower limits of normal. I'm reasonably certain that he'll catch up nicely when he reaches your home and grow within the normal range.

His lab tests showed a weakly positive hepatitis B surface antibody which may be due to his immunizations. He also had a weakly positive hepatitis B e antibody which could either be a false positive or be antibody transferred from his birth mother prior to birth. The most important test was the hepatitis B surface antigen which was negative so he doesn't have hepatitis B. He also tested negative for HIV and syphilis.

His development is close to being normal for his given age. Again, it may be completely normal for his actual age if he was a bit premature or they miscalculated his chronological age. Again, I'm optimistic that he'll catch-up once he reaches your home.

His atrial septal defect (hole between the two minor pumping chambers of the heart) is very small and should resolve spontaneously. I agree that all he needs is another echo in about 12 months. The only other issue is a mild anemia which is common in China. Iron supplementation once you return (if it's still low) will likely take care of the problem. Overall, I'm optimistic about his future in your home.

As our adoption process for Charlie propelled forward, we were still deeply mourning our loss of Daniel, but slowly the Lord began to fill our holes of pain and anguish. He replaced them with joy all over again — the excitement of a new family member to love

– one with a hole in his heart that would symbolize his big brother, Daniel, looking down upon him.

The holidays, Christmas especially, weren't without struggle and they were very tough for our family. I wrote this blog post when the holiday feeling started to kick in and the stark reality of our loss had grabbed me by the throat:

PAIN IN THE MIDST OF JOY | November 14, 2010

Tonight as we sat down to dinner, Madi and Daddy insisted on music. I tuned in to the holiday music channel, and then it hit me like a ton of bricks:

Daniel won't be coming home for Christmas.

We won't get the picture on Santa's lap with Madi laughing and Daniel crying his eyes out.

He won't get to help decorate the house and break a few ornaments.

He won't get to watch Frosty and Rudolph and all those other Christmas classics.

He won't get to dance around the house singing "Jingle Bells" with Madi and Daddy.

He won't get to drive around to "oooh" and "ahhh" at the beautiful lights.

He won't get the joy of meeting Matthew, his cousin, for the first time.

He won't get to see the beautiful stocking that Aunt Sheila knitted for him by hand.

He won't know the awesome smell of a real Christmas tree.

We won't get to make Christmas cookies together (okay... that's a stretch and probably wouldn't happen anyway, but it's fun to think about)

We won't see the joy on his face after his first visit from Santa.

As I sit in my puddle of tears, I am going to try to re-focus on what Daniel *will* see for Christmas.

He will see Jesus. He will be sitting right there on His Lap enjoying every moment.

Daniel will be listening to the choir of angels, and he will see the brightest lights we can ever imagine.

Daniel *will be Home* for Christmas.

And he will be watching us... missing him.

We hung Daniel's stocking up with the rest, and Madi promptly filled it with a few special things: her brother's favorite dress, his favorite headband of hers, and his favorite stuffed toy, "Baby Girl." Madi's preschool director, Peggie (who became a dear friend), gave us the fabulous idea of requesting written memories or stories about Daniel from family members, friends, and those he had touched.

Our greatest Christmas gift was the love stuffed into that stocking – an outpouring of beautiful heartfelt sentiments and memories about our son – some we had forgotten about, and some we never even knew about. It was the perfect gift to fill our hearts with joy that Christmas, and we plan to preserve those keepsakes for Madi and Charlie to reflect on together someday.

Just before we traveled back to China for Charlie, Daniel finally came to me in a dream. Actually, I think I should refer to it as a "visitation." When I mentioned it to Jimmy the next morning, he informed me that I had been giggling in my sleep. The tears became uncontrollable, and I knew that Daniel had been with me. In my dream, Jimmy and I had gone into the orphanage (it looked more like a hospital) looking for Charlie, and came upon Daniel's familiar little face in the crowd. He was in a wheelchair and his hands and feet were wrapped up in bandages. Our son had aged only a little, and we clearly knew it was him.

As we approached Daniel, he looked up at me and said, "Mama!" We were so thrilled to see him, and we knew instantly that he would be leaving with us. I was excited to tell him that I had Juice Plus+® gummies for him, and he squealed with delight. We continued to look for Charlie in the orphanage, but had difficulty identifying him. I'm sure that confused feeling stemmed from the fact that we hadn't received any updated photos of Charlie since November, and his appearance at the time was somewhat of a mystery to us. But I just remember feeling so profoundly warm having found Daniel.

The dream went on for a while but, sadly, many of the details escape me now. What didn't escape me, however, was how I felt the morning after as I reflected upon the dream – it seemed so real, and I felt as if I'd truly seen him and had him back for a while. I find it significant that his hands and feet were bandaged. For I believe it was a sign that Daniel had carried his cross and is now with Jesus. That thought warmed me to the core.

Chapter Thirty-Two

SHOW HOPE

Many families in the adoption world may know about Show Hope, yet we weren't aware of their good will until we began our adoption process to bring Daniel home. Show Hope is a non-profit organization that mobilizes individuals and communities to meet the most pressing needs of orphans in distress. They do this by both providing homes for waiting children through adoption aid grants, as well as life-saving medical care for orphans with special needs. (Source: www.showhope.org)

Originally established in 2003 as Shaohannah's Hope by musician Steven Curtis Chapman and his wife, Mary Beth, Show Hope was initially founded out of their desire to see more children find their way into forever families. Though many families they talked to were willing to adopt, the financial costs of adoption were simply too high. Named after the Chapman's first adopted daughter, Shaohannah Hope Chapman, Shaohannah's Hope has grown far beyond the initial vision of helping a few orphans find homes.

Since 2009, after changing the name to Show Hope, this organization has seen an amazing explosion in growth. From a six-story caring facility in China that is equipped to provide surgeries and medical care to special needs orphans, to multiplying the effects of the adoption grant program by assisting churches in setting up their own adoption funds, Show Hope continues to expand its remarkable worldwide impact.

As Steven Curtis Chapman's heart for China grew more and more through his family's two adoptions of Shaohannah and Stevey Joy, he continued to visit China to minister there through music. After leading worship at Beijing International Christian Fellowship on Easter Sunday in April of 2004, he left through the back door and ran into some missionaries who let him hold one of their Chinese babies. When Steven asked if she was theirs, they said no, but they were trying to find a home for her. He asked, "What is her name?" They said, "Maria." Immediately, a song Steven wrote years ago, called, "Who's Gonna Love Maria," started playing in his head. Steven couldn't believe the coincidence of her name and was shaken to the core. While thinking about this, he broke down in tears and then called his wife, explaining the strong connection he'd made with this little girl named Maria. When Steven posed the thought to Mary Beth that they were meant to adopt her, she jokingly responded by saying, "Well, she better play an instrument because she will be going on the road with you."

Steven couldn't get Maria of his mind, but he certainly had not planned to adopt another child. Because Maria was a special needs child and was already placed with an agency in a special needs program, Steven thought that maybe they were just supposed to help her find a home. But when he returned to the States, Mary Beth already had the paperwork out and said, "I think we're supposed to go and get Maria."

The pieces fell into place, and a couple months after Steven had met that little orphaned girl in Beijing, he once again returned to China to pick up Maria Sue Chunxi Chapman. She had a heart condition, which classified her as "special needs," but the Chapmans have a different idea of why she was special: she was theirs. Before they completed the adoption, she was re-diagnosed as being healthy, and her healthy heart began to constantly overflow into the hearts of those around her. As the youngest of the family, she was certainly a handful, but Steven and Mary Beth knew that their family would never have been complete without her.

For four years, the Chapmans grew together through laughter and tears, joy and pain. And on May 21, 2008, an unspeakable tragedy struck the Chapman household as Maria Sue Chunxi Chapman was rushed to the hospital after having been accidentally hit by a car in the family's driveway. She passed away that day and saw her eternal adoption at last finalized, as Maria's Heavenly Father took her home to be with Him.

In their daughter's memory, they built "Maria's Big House of Hope" in Luoyang, China – one of the three Special Care Centers that is supported in China by Show Hope. In addition, they have also seen the ministry that they founded (just nine years ago) help over 3,000 waiting orphans find their forever families. Together they have seen Steven's career reach a record 56 Dove Awards (more Dove Awards than any other artist to date), five GRAMMY awards, 46 #1 songs so far, and over ten million records sold.

In Chapter One, I mentioned how Aunt Karen (Grandma Pauline's sister in Georgia) had attended one of Steven Curtis Chapman's concerts in January, 2008 and learned of their generous organization. It is interesting to me that even after Aunt Karen had provided us with this incredible resource, during our adoption process with Daniel I just didn't feel in my heart that we truly needed financial assistance. When I had started writing a letter to Show Hope in August, 2008, I never finished the application and – instead – Jimmy and I drained a savings account to bring Daniel home and meet the insurance deductible for his heart surgery. Needless to say, it was worth every single penny.

This time, however, when I wrote our letter of application to Show Hope requesting financial assistance, we knew that we really needed their help. We also knew that the Chapman family would understand exactly how we felt, since they had experienced the devastating loss of their precious daughter, Maria.

One of the requirements on our Show Hope application was a statement of faith from both Jimmy and me. Jimmy, who is such an emotional person (but one who tends to keep it under wraps) just blew me away when I read his testimony. Instead of holding back, he'd poured his heart out on paper. Here is Jimmy's beautifully written statement of faith that brought tears to my eyes:

Jimmy's statement of faith

My journey towards finding my faith started when my wife and I began the process to adopt our first daughter from China in 2006. We searched many churches and finally found the perfect home that was right under our nose, and it was filled with our friends and acquaintances. We started attending St. Vincent Ferrer Catholic Church, and it was the perfect fit to revive our faith. We entered into the RCIA program and as each class ended, we realized how much we were missing in God. The congregation accepted us with open hearts and arms, as if we were already family. It was fantastic to feel so close to God.

We brought our beautiful daughter, Madi, home on a Thursday, and that Sunday we made our first family trip to church. Madi, as well as we, love that Sunday Mass brings us closer to God. We realized how deep our faith was when we brought our son Daniel home from China last February. Daniel had Tetralogy of Fallot and needed open-heart surgery.

We were confident that God would guide us and protect us through this surgery. Daniel's operation (on May 11th) was successful, but his lungs became an issue and many other problems arose. One evening, very late at night, we were called into the hospital for an emergency procedure. My wife, Lisa, and I called our closest family members and friends, but no one answered.

We realized this was part of God's plan to prepare us that, no matter what happened, He had a greater plan for Daniel. Earlier, people all over the world had been brought together for prayer chains in Daniel's name. And some who had distanced themselves from God were now getting closer because of this little boy and our strength in our faith. That night, as we walked the empty halls of the hospital, we realized the possibility that God had another plan for Daniel as much as we wanted him to stay with us. We began to realize there was a strong possibility that he would not come out of the hospital alive. We shared a feeling of calmness and warmth knowing that if he were called to Heaven, he was where we all want to be someday.

Daniel passed away on May 30th. It was Trinity Sunday. We saw this as a beautiful sign that Daniel had spread the word of the Lord, and it was his time. We will never truly understand why the plan was put in place, but we know that Daniel touched a lot of people and also solidified our faith as we found comfort in the saddest day of our life.

We have now been matched with another beautiful boy from China who has a small hole in his heart. With the love of family, friends, and God, we know he will be safe. We are thankful that Daniel is watching over him, and watching over our family, as well. Faith will forever be the most important rock for this family.

Five days before our departure to China to bring our son, Charlie, home, we received the wonderful news that Show Hope had granted our request and had chosen to provide financial assistance for our adoption, as they generously do for so many families who ask for their help. Through the generosity of friends and family, along with Show Hope's grant assistance and our adoption tax credit for our sweet Daniel, God had provided for our new adoption almost down to the dollar.

♡

Chapter Thirty-Three

BACK TO CHINA

In March, 2011, we traveled to Shanghai, China to bring home our second son. On this journey, we were not accompanied by our parents. Jimmy and I joked that it was finally time to do this journey on our own – without parental supervision. Bubba and Grandpa had accompanied us to bring Madi home. And Grandpa Murphy had shared such a special journey to bring Daniel home that he decided to stay back this time.

The best part was that, thanks to all of the financial support we'd received, big sister Madi was able to travel to China with us, and it was priceless to have her take part in such a life-changing event. She was a breath of fresh air to travel with (believe it or not, at five years of age), and there were even a few times in which she acted as "the voice of reason" for Jimmy and me!

As we waited to board our flight for Shanghai on St. Patrick's Day, I simultaneously felt so many conflicting emotions: elated, terrified, excited, anxious, and hopeful – all bundled up into one. Jimmy and I opted to skip the leg to Beijing this time since we'd been sightseeing there twice before. We flew directly to Shanghai and spent a few days relaxing in the hotel and adjusting to the time change, especially for Madi's sake. The cold and rainy weather cooperated with our plan to chill out indoors, and we were a well-rested family when it was time to meet Charlie. I'm certain there was much more sightseeing in Shanghai than one could imagine, but our focus was not on touring – it was all about family bonding.

We were, for unknown reasons, denied a visit to the orphanage, so our "Gotcha Day" moment took place on Monday morning at the Ministry of Civil Affairs. As the taxi drove us over to meet our son for the first time, my husband and I felt the familiar twinge of simultaneous nervousness and excitement. The ministry staff led us to a room where we sat for about half an hour preparing for our union and scurrying about to prepare both the still and the video cameras. I didn't want a single moment to go unrecorded. Our union with Charlie was indescribable. In the wake of such a significantly traumatic time in our lives – less than one year later – God had just provided us with another miracle to behold.

Charlie's Gotcha Day

The officials handed us a baby who was much smaller than we expected. He was busy eating a chocolate covered biscuit at the time, and the officials instructed us to "give him cookies if he cries," which wasn't exactly part of our parenting plan. Charlie seemed to be a very sweet and quiet baby who didn't complain much at all. We noticed that he was visibly emotionally detached, and he would barely make eye contact with any of us. Charlie seemed unphased by the whole transition, and we realized that – unlike our bonding process with Madi, who had been in foster care and bonded to us immediately, and Daniel who had grown close to his caretakers – Charlie actually needed to *learn how* to attach. That would probably be our family's largest hurdle. We also noticed right away that Charlie was a self-soother who would constantly stick the two middle fingers of his left hand into his mouth. He even had two hard calluses on those fingers, which indicated that he'd truly been in self-soothing mode quite a bit.

Charlie was a tiny thing, which we didn't quite grasp even though we knew about it from his updates. We nicknamed him "Peanut" pretty much right away. At 18 months old, Charlie was swimming in 12-month clothing, and we had to roll the waistline of his pants down two and three times! Reports indicated that he'd been given a limited amount of solid foods during the course of each day, and – based on his tiny stature – we could see that the bulk of his nutrition had come from his four small bottle feedings of formula per day.

Jimmy and I could hardly wait to remedy this knowing that his little body simply needed to be introduced to solid foods on a regular basis. Since he only had four teeth on both top and bottom, I opted to sneak him Juice Plus+® by opening our capsules and emptying them into his formula. It worked like a charm. Because Charlie had spent much of his time in a walker (and likely his crib, primarily), his leg muscles were very poorly developed and he wasn't walking yet. He wasn't standing on his own without assistance either – but we knew that would come with practice.

The three of us enjoyed our time in Shanghai getting to know our new family member. Jimmy and I found ourselves in the background when we needed to be, allowing Madi to fully embrace her new little brother and giving him a chance to warm up to her, too. She was over the moon and loved the fact that – even though he was already 18 months old – Charlie was still very much a little baby.

After we finalized our adoption and completed all of the necessary steps within Shanghai (which took four more days), we were finally able to fly to Guangzhou to complete the last leg of our mission. The evening that we walked back into the White Swan Hotel in Guangzhou was bittersweet for us.

As Jimmy approached the front desk to check in, I decided to stroll around the lobby a bit with Madi when I heard a familiar tune coming from the lobby bar. I couldn't imagine a more apropos song for that moment – it was Eric Clapton's "Tears in Heaven," written about his young son who had died. I instantly felt a stabbing sadness from the sharp pains of my own loss, and I secretly wept – hoping that Madi wouldn't notice – as we paced the dark lobby hand in hand. It was such a sweet reminder of our Daniel who, only a year earlier, had been with us in that very same hotel. It was surreal – both painfully sad and abundantly joyful – all at the same time.

While in Guangzhou, we visited our faithful Christian shopkeeper, Jordan. He remembered our precious Daniel, and his eyes filled with tears as we told him the fate of our little "Lucky Link." Jordan offered us a drawing for Charlie's name in Chinese characters complete with translation, the same as he had done for Daniel. Next to Charles, he painted "Glory," and next to Stanley, he painted "Victory." That pretty much summed it up for us – our "Lucky Link" brought us "Glory and Victory" through the name of Jesus Christ, our Lord.

This time, our family attended Mass in Our Lady of Lourdes Catholic Church, the same church that Jimmy and I had entered by ourselves the year before during our stay with Daniel. The parishioners stared at us in a way that was overtly benevolent – as if they recognized that we were in China to adopt one of their own and felt grateful for it. There was standing room only in the small sanctuary, but an elderly woman jumped up and gave us her seat in the last pew so that we could sit down. What juxtaposition from our western culture where it is customary to give up our seats for the elderly! Her unexpected gesture felt awkward, but we could see that she really wanted to be hospitable, so we complied. It was a special moment for our family, once again, to feel the love of humanity in a place that seemed a million miles away from home.

The three of us took Charlie for the all-too-familiar medical exam in Guangzhou, too. Fortunately, our government (as I mentioned in Chapter Seven) had changed the immunization requirements, and we were able to leave the clinic without any vaccinations at all. Charlie's vaccinations had all been administered and well documented back at his orphanage in Shanghai.

In the last of Charlie's three exams, Jimmy and I encountered a bit of a scare when the doctor pressed his stethoscope tightly to Charlie's chest and listened for several minutes. My husband and I paid close attention to the expression on the doctor's face. Then in broken Chinglish (Chinese combined with English), he asked, "Has the baby had any surgeries?" to which Jimmy replied with concern, "No."

He then waved us to another room – a special room that seemed to be designated for medical problems and inconsistencies. We remembered that room vividly – we had been in there the year before with Daniel. In our state of panic, we motioned for our guide to come into the room and translate for us. They bantered back and forth while we watched two more physicians parade through and take turns listening to Charlie's heart. Jimmy and I could barely stand the tension.

Finally, to our amazement, our guide turned to us and uttered the sweet word that we never dreamed we'd hear: "NORMAL." The doctors could not detect *any* sign of a heart defect. And since we've been back home, we've received this same opinion from two American medical professionals – one of them a pediatric cardiologist. Praise the Lord.

We had experienced another incredible adoption journey. But we, once again, could not wait to give up the "fantasy life" of a fully-prepared buffet breakfast every morning and a work-free leisurely schedule to just race home and return to reality. The night before we departed from Guangzhou, I wrote our final blog post before we headed home.

A NOTE TO DANIEL | April 1, 2011

You did it, buddy. Soon after you left us for Heaven, you planted a seed in Mommy and Daddy to come back to China and bring another child into our family. So we did. We followed our hearts and God's plan, and here we are with your little brother, Charlie. We are now a family of four, plus an angel. We will never, ever forget you. You will always be our first little boy whose spirit was brighter than the sun. We promise to take very good care of Charlie, and we will think of you so often as we watch him grow. He will know all about his big brother and what an amazing little soul you were here on this Earth.

Thank you, Daniel, for teaching us so much about love and about life. Thank you for seeing us through on another divine mission of faith. We thank God for the months you were in our life, and we will love you forever, our precious son.

Chapter Thirty-Four

LUCKY LINK

$\mathcal{I}$ mentioned, in Chapter Seven, how Daniel was named our "Lucky Link" by a faithful Christian shopkeeper in Guangzhou, China. And now – in retrospect – we feel as if Daniel truly was a "Lucky Link" in our family. He is our link between Heaven and Earth, and he was the connection that brought us to Charlie less than one year after his passing.

Charlie's actions, as he approached and passed the two-year mark, sometimes remind us so much of Daniel's. It is hard to explain precisely how we feel inside when we see these resemblances. There is still sadness at having lost Daniel, but at the same time we feel such incredible joy to have Charlie in our family as we watch him slowly come out of his shell. Ultimately, the bitterness and loss are outweighed by sweetness and joy from knowing that Charlie is with our family *because of* Daniel, which is just another reason we thank God for our "Lucky Link." We were given the opportunity to love him, and now we also get to love Charlie *because of him.*

Since day one of having Charlie home, he has been continually drawn to the plaque of Daniel in our backyard. I'm not exaggerating. And on a couple of occasions, strange things have happened that have made us think he personally knows our "Lucky Link."

One evening in June, I carried Charlie outside to put something on the grill. We walked across the yard over to the plaque, and we did our standard ritual. I said hello to Daniel, and Charlie touched his face. But then I just stood there for a minute. Suddenly, the wind kicked up out of nowhere and blew the bamboo plant behind the plaque while Grandma's bell started ringing like crazy. Charlie looked down the yard towards our gate, and stared as if he were fixated on something – or someone. Then, he reached out his arm and hand. Okay, I suppose that's typical behavior for a baby. But then he turned back to the plaque and reached out to Daniel's face as if to say, "That's the same little guy I see right there!" He did this a couple of times before we went back into the house. Call me delusional, or wishful maybe, but it sure made me wonder if Charlie saw his big brother.

On another occasion (just a couple months later), Charlie and I were enjoying an outdoor breeze in the backyard one evening, and it happened again. He suddenly crouched down and peered between the slats of our wooden deck railing, and his gaze was fastened to the plaque. After a moment, Charlie quickly got up, took a couple of steps backward, and looked totally mesmerized as he stared in that direction. A breeze kicked up, and without hesitation, Charlie made a beeline down the step and into the yard. I knew exactly where he was headed.

Brothers

He barreled through the grass in the direction of the plaque, and with his tender bare feet he timidly made his way through the mulch. When he'd reached his destination, Charlie held out his little fingers and touched Daniel's face. I had no doubt, once again, that his eyes saw something (or someone) that mine couldn't.

As I conclude this chapter of our story, I know it is just the beginning of a new start for our family. The profound imprint that Daniel made on our lives is everlasting, and we've come full circle in so many ways. In over a year's time, it's hard to believe how much we've changed as a family, especially spiritually.

And it's interesting to us how God can warp time. Though Daniel was with our family for only four short months, it seems as if he were with us forever. We are so deeply grateful for that. What we have learned through our open-heart experience with Daniel is that love has nothing to do with a calendar. Those 127 days with Daniel touched us as deeply as if he'd been with us for decades. Though one of our deepest regrets is that we did not get the chance to share years with him instead of months, every moment he spent with us – and with others – immeasurably enhanced our hearts and our lives. We never thought that *losing* Daniel was an option. We had every hope – the doctors had every hope – that he would not only make it, but that he would thrive. Daniel's body appeared strong, but his will was even stronger. The bottom line is that pain is pain and love is love, because – in this life – there is no yardstick with which to measure emotional intensity. It's amazing how this little person came into our lives and touched us so profoundly. He taught us so much. Our hearts are so much fuller, and we carry him in our souls every minute of the day.

Would we do it again? Yes, we absolutely would. Because having Daniel was worth every minute of our pain. Are there rough times? *Without a doubt.* But we are eternally grateful for those rough times because they are attached to having been blessed with Daniel's presence. Even in our darkest hour, we could still see the light. With every milestone missed, our hearts break all over again as we wonder what kind of person he would be today, but our painful emotions are always overshadowed by the sheer gratitude of having had Daniel in our lives. His precious face is still on the refrigerators of some – providing inspiration and hope, joyful hope of our own salvation someday.

Jimmy, Madi and I wouldn't trade a second of our time with Daniel, even though we lost him to our Lord. We are forever changed because of him, and we are forever better and richer because of how Daniel touched our lives. We are so eternally thankful that our son knew the love of a family on this earth. Daniel did not die an orphan – he did not die alone. So we live out our days with Daniel as our son, but also as our angel. And though we are sad that he didn't get to experience more "earthly" things as *we* know them, Jimmy and I have faith that our son has received his just reward in the Kingdom of Heaven, where we all hope to end up someday. I don't believe it gets any better than that.

Daniel serves as proof that *we never know* what God is going to hand us, and we need to cherish *every single moment*. We all have a purpose on this Earth, and many times we ask ourselves why things happen that aren't according to our plan. And as hard as we might try to seek them out, we'll never know the answers to those questions – at least not here and now.

I passed by a nearby church recently and read a sign that resonated deeply within me. "Thank God, not only for the roses, but also for the thorns." Just think about that for a moment; we are supposed to be as grateful for the difficult times as we are for the joyful ones. Pretty tough stuff to swallow at times – but it is true. From our family's perspective, we have realized that sometimes it is *in the sharpest of thorns* that you really feel God's presence *the most*. It is in our darkest hours that we, as humans, are truly Divinely Embraced, if only we open our hearts and allow God to come inside.

We hope that our family's story has inspired you to hug your children a little tighter each day, take more time to smell the roses, and embrace each moment a whole lot more. It's important to remember that each of us, while here on Earth, has a life that is truly precious and packed full of unknowns. It is also our sincere hope that you will keep your heart open – so that you may hear when the Holy Spirit whispers to *you*.

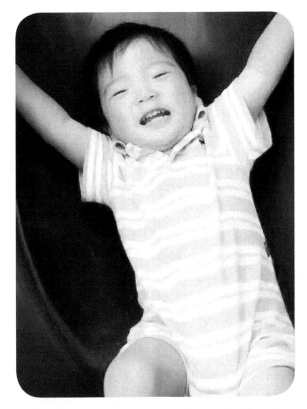

"And in the end, it's not the years in a life, it's the life in the years."
— Abraham Lincoln

NOTES FROM THE AUTHOR

It's hard to believe that as of this revised edition of *With an Open Heart*, it has been over five years without having our son with us physically. Writing this book was a huge part of my grieving process. God is the true author of our family's story, which is still being written, and I am grateful to the Holy Spirit for prompting me to write about our little boy.

Although Daniel's journey on this earth was short, it is our belief that he came with a great mission. It is our desire to continue sharing our little angel with the world and hope that his life will continue to touch others in the same way he touched us. I have learned so much since his passing.

After our son's death, I became very involved with social media networking, blog-stalking, Yahoo groups, and Facebook groups. All of the support and medical resources that we really needed before we adopted Daniel, we found after. This was hard to digest, but because I believe that everything happens for a reason, I must stay the course. I feel blessed to be continuously "armed" with more resources and will share them with others as I learn about them. For the sake of other children, I am thankful they exist.

I've also connected with many amazing people who've taught me the real definition of bravery and selflessness – people who've stepped out of their "comfortable" lives and have leaped to adopt terminally ill children just to give them a chance to live. I've come to know children who've been steps away from death and have fought to survive – some of them given new life through the miracle of organ transplantation.

I have also realized that miracles come in many forms – while I've watched countless beautiful children find their healing miracles here on earth, I've watched others find their miracle in eternal life, like our Daniel. And there's peace in realizing that – while terribly painful for those left behind – eternal life should be viewed as a miracle, too.

My eyes and my heart have been opened to the plight of the orphan and call of adoption more passionately than they were before. My faith is stronger than ever, and I believe that was one of the rainbows that came with the storm. I praise the Lord for each and every blessing.

Ultimately, we lost our son. But we are so grateful to have loved him and to have been given the gift of time with his sweet soul. How blessed we are that – even though it was for such a short time – God entrusted us as Daniel's loving family before He called our son Home to Heaven. Years after our little one has passed on, so much beauty has been birthed from his existence, and Daniel's red thread is still very much woven into our lives. He is the gift that transformed us forever – that *truly* opened our hearts.

With all my heart,
Lisa

IN CLOSING

By Deacon Lee Levenson

The story that has lovingly unfolded in Lisa Murphy's beautifully written narrative is more than just a moving book about a loving family's journey to China, and their adoption of Daniel – a toddler who was challenged from birth with serious health issues.

This child was born as Weifeng Hong in Nanchang, China, and suffered from a serious, life-threatening heart condition. He was abandoned by his birth mother and placed into the institutional care of the Chinese government. If not for the loving intervention of Lisa and Jim Murphy, it is almost certain that he would have languished in an institutional setting. Because of his medical condition, Weifeng Hong would probably have perished there as an orphan.

Certainly, this is a story about a loving family's adoption journey of compassion, caring and hope. But, above all, this book is a moving narrative about optimism in the face of personal tragedy, the strength provided by an overwhelming faith in God's providence, and triumph over adversity.

Many of Lisa and Jim's friends and family were as understandably devastated at the loss of this beautiful little boy as I was. Not surprisingly, some people openly asked why God would allow this to happen. As to His reasons, none of us can truly understand, but (hopefully) we will one day have the opportunity to ask God ourselves. We must simply trust in Him.

Still, as I struggled to address these difficult issues in preparation for the homily for Daniel's Mass of the Angels, I turned to His Word in Sacred Scripture. I found some answers in Ezekiel Chapter 36. In verse 24, we read, "For I will take you away from among the nations, gather you from all the foreign lands..." and in verse 26, "I will give you a new heart and place a new spirit within you, taking from your bodies your stony hearts and giving you natural hearts." Then, in verse 25, "I will sprinkle clean water upon you to cleanse you from all your impurities...."

Little Weifeng Hong was "gathered from...the foreign lands" by the wonderful Murphy family – who traveled halfway around the world to embrace him. They not only brought him lovingly into their family, they also gave him a terrific sister, Madi, as well as loving grandparents, aunts, uncles, cousins and friends.

The Murphys brought Daniel to the Baptismal font where he was born again into the life of Jesus Christ. Then, together with a dedicated team of medical professionals, Lisa and Jim gave Daniel a chance to overcome his serious medical issues. Sadly, despite everyone's efforts, it was not to be; Daniel was called home to Heaven. But, blessedly, not before he knew love, laughter and family. Daniel was able to come into the light of Christ, play, laugh, and experience the joy of a loving, caring and faith-filled family.

As Saint Paul wrote in 1 Corinthians, "Love is patient, love is kind...it does not brood over injury...It bears all things, believes all things, hopes all things, endures all things…So faith, hope, love remain, these three, but the greatest of these is love."

Lisa and Jim Murphy, together with their daughter, Madi, and now, with little Charlie, (as well as all of their family and supportive friends) beautifully exhibit the above words from Saint Paul. As you've read Lisa's words and learned about Daniel's journey, I hope you allow Saint Paul's exhortation that the greatest of these is love resonate in your own heart.

With an Open Heart serves as a reminder that perhaps there is a child out there who is waiting for you – or someone close to you – and needs you to embrace this notion, as well.

May God bless you and keep you and your loved ones in His embrace always.

In Christ Jesus,
Deacon Lee Levenson
St. Vincent Ferrer Catholic Church
Delray Beach, FL

ACKNOWLEDGMENTS

(Updated for revised edition)

$\mathcal{S}aying$ "thank you" just doesn't seem sufficient for the many people who touched our lives during our blessed time with Daniel. Our family members and friends were so involved in our adoption process, our bonding process, and our grieving process. To each and every one of you – you know who you are – thank you for loving Daniel, and please know that we appreciate everything you did and continue to do for us. Whether or not you are mentioned in this book, you were an important part of Daniel's life, and we are forever grateful for your love and support. We also acknowledge that so many of you still remain nameless and unknown to our family. Please know that we are grateful to have been lifted up in your prayers.

Most importantly, thank you to our ever-loving and eternal Father for giving us Daniel. Thank you for opening our eyes and our hearts to answer the call to adopt your children. We have been blessed beyond measure, and it is only because of your saving grace that we receive such precious gifts. We are forever humbled and grateful for your unfailing mercy upon us.

To Anj and Michelle, thank you for your faith in this project and for your vision to see it through. This revised edition would not be nearly as beautiful without your perfect cover and interior design and honest (and spiritual) feedback. I am thankful for both of you, my sisters-in-Christ.

To the ladies sent by the Holy Spirit at the last minute – Dardi and Nikki, thank you for taking time to perfect the final copy. It would not be the same without you and your loving efforts.

To the Petro Princesses for your friendship and kindness, Princess Averie will always be remembered in our home, and we imagine that, up in Heaven, she is showering many children, including Daniel, with her love.

To all of you reading this memoir, we thank you for taking time to know our son. We hope and pray that Daniel's life has in some way touched yours, and that his story will inspire you to live, listen, and leap with an open heart.

ABOUT THE AUTHORS

LISA MURPHY is a Christian writer, blogger, school and parish volunteer, independent sales distributor for Juice Plus+® products, and adoption advocate, but her most valued post is being a stay-at-home mom to her three beautiful children. Lisa resides in Delray Beach, Florida with her husband, Jim, and their children, Madi, Charlie, and Joseph. One of Lisa's passions in life is to make a difference in their son Daniel's memory, and to keep him alive by sharing his inspiring story with others.

Murphy family

MARILYN MURRAY WILLISON is an accomplished author of six non-fiction books and has worked as a respected international journalist in both the U.S. and the U.K. Marilyn also served as health and fitness editor of the *Los Angeles Times Syndicate*. As an adoptee, author, and mother, *With an Open Heart* spoke to her on a variety of levels.

Marilyn Murray Willison

APPENDIX

The Battle Hymn of the Republic

Mine eyes have seen the glory of the coming of the Lord:
He is trampling out the vintage
where the grapes of wrath are stored;
He hath loosed the fateful lightning of His terrible swift sword:
His truth is marching on.

Glory, glory, hallelujah!
Glory, glory, hallelujah!
Glory, glory, hallelujah!
His truth is marching on.

I have seen Him in the watch-fires of a hundred circling camps,
They have builded Him an altar in the evening dews and damps;
I can read His righteous sentence by the dim and flaring lamps:
His day is marching on.

Glory, glory, hallelujah!
Glory, glory, hallelujah!
Glory, glory, hallelujah!
His day is marching on.

I have read a fiery gospel writ in burnished rows of steel:
"As ye deal with my contemners, so with you my grace shall deal;
Let the Hero, born of woman, crush the serpent with his heel,
Since God is marching on."

Glory, glory, hallelujah!
Glory, glory, hallelujah!
Glory, glory, hallelujah!
Since God is marching on.

He has sounded forth the trumpet that shall never call retreat;
He is sifting out the hearts of men before His judgment-seat:
Oh, be swift, my soul, to answer Him!
Be jubilant, my feet!
Our God is marching on.

Glory, glory, hallelujah!
Glory, glory, hallelujah!
Glory, glory, hallelujah!
Our God is marching on.

In the beauty of the lilies Christ was born across the sea,
With a glory in His bosom that transfigures you and me:
As He died to make men holy, let us die to make men free,
While God is marching on.

Glory, glory, hallelujah!
Glory, glory, hallelujah!
Glory, glory, hallelujah!
While God is marching on.

He is coming like the glory of the morning on the wave,
He is Wisdom to the mighty, He is Succour to the brave,
So the world shall be His footstool, and the soul of Time His slave,
Our God is marching on.

Glory, glory, hallelujah!
Glory, glory, hallelujah!
Glory, glory, hallelujah!
Our God is marching on.

Psalms Chapter 91 - King James Version
(given to me by nurse Joy)

1 He that dwelleth in the secret place of the most High
shall abide under the shadow of the Almighty.

2 I will say of the LORD, [He is] my refuge and my fortress:
my God; in him will I trust.

3 Surely he shall deliver thee from the snare of the fowler,
[and] from the noisome pestilence.

4 He shall cover thee with his feathers, and under his wings shalt thou
trust: his truth [shall be thy] shield and buckler.

5 Thou shalt not be afraid for the terror by night;
[nor] for the arrow [that] flieth by day;

6 [Nor] for the pestilence [that] walketh in darkness;
[nor] for the destruction [that] wasteth at noonday.

7 A thousand shall fall at thy side, and ten thousand
at thy right hand; [but] it shall not come nigh thee.

8 Only with thine eyes shalt thou behold
and see the reward of the wicked.

9 Because thou hast made the LORD, [which is] my refuge,
[even] the most High, thy habitation;

10 There shall no evil befall thee,
neither shall any plague come nigh thy dwelling.

11 For he shall give his angels charge over thee,
to keep thee in all thy ways.

12 They shall bear thee up in [their] hands,
lest thou dash thy foot against a stone.

13 Thou shalt tread upon the lion and adder:
the young lion and the dragon shalt thou trample under feet.

14 Because he hath set his love upon me, therefore will I deliver him:
I will set him on high, because he hath known my name.

15 He shall call upon me, and I will answer him:
I [will be] with him in trouble; I will deliver him, and honour him.

16 With long life will I satisfy him, and shew him my salvation.

RESOURCES & ORGANIZATIONS

HALF THE SKY FOUNDATION
715 Hearst Avenue, Ste. 200
Berkeley, CA 94710
Phone: (510) 525-3377
www.halfthesky.org

HOLT INTERNATIONAL CHILDREN'S SERVICES
P.O. Box 2880
1195 City View | Eugene, OR 97402
Phone: (541) 687-2202 | Fax: (541) 683-6175
www.holtinternational.org
info@holtinternational.org

JUICE PLUS +® NUTRITIONAL PRODUCTS
lisamurphy.juiceplus.com

LITTLE HEARTS MEDICAL
Helps children born with congenital heart disease. Families considering the adoption of a child from China born with CHD may contact LHM for a cardiac case summary, free of charge
Andrea Olson, Executive Director
29514 NE Hammond Court
Battle Ground, WA 98604
Phone: (503) 999-5718
aolson@littleheartsmedical.org
www.littleheartsmedical.org

MORNING STAR FOUNDATION
Cares for orphans with complex heart disease and partners with families to help provide the medical care their children desperately need.
Meredith Toering, International Director
meredith@morningstarproject.org
www.morningstarproject.org

PEOPLE IN CRISIS UNITED
12555 Biscayne Blvd. Suite 904
Miami, FL 33181-2597
Phone: (786) 252-3466
peopleincrisisunited@gmail.com

RONALD MCDONALD HOUSE CHARITIES-SOUTH FLORIDA
1145 NW 14th Terrace
Miami, FL 33136
Phone: (305) 324-5683 | Fax: (305) 324-5689
www.rmhcsouthflorida.org
rmhmiami@rmhcsouthflorida.org

SHOW HOPE
PO Box 647
Franklin, TN 37065
Phone: (615) 550-5600 Fax: (615) 595-0850
www.showhope.org

ST. VINCENT FERRER CATHOLIC CHURCH
840 George Bush Boulevard
Delray Beach, FL 33483
Phone: (561) 276-6892 Fax: (561) 276-8068
www.stvincentferrer.com

UNIVERSITY OF MINNESOTA DEPARTMENT OF PEDIATRICS
International Adoption Medicine Program & Clinic (adoption file review)
717 Delaware St SE, 3rd Floor
Mail Code 1932, Room 365
Minneapolis, MN 55455
Phone: (612) 624-1164 | Fax: (612) 625-2920
iac@umn.edu

30240688R00162

Made in the USA
Middletown, DE
17 March 2016